Dinah Zike's

Big Book of
Science

Grade Levels K-6

Dinah Zike, M.Ed.

Copyright 2004, Dinah-Might Adventures, LP
Dinah-Might Adventures, LP
P.O. Box 690328
San Antonio, Texas 78269-0328

Office (210) 698-0123
Fax (210) 698-0095
Orders only: 1-800-99DINAH (993-4624)
Orders or catalog requests: orders@dinah.com
E-mail: dma@dinah.com
Website: www.dinah.com
ISBN Number: 1-882796-23-3

Table of Contents

Science Graphics

Dear Teacher:

What is a Foldable?

In this book you will find instructions for making Foldables as well as ideas on how to use them. A Foldable is a 3-D, interactive graphic organizer. Making a Foldable gives students a fun, hands-on activity that helps them organize and retain information.

I first began inventing, designing, and adapting Foldables over thirty years ago. Today, I present Foldable workshops and keynote addresses to over 50,000 teachers and parents a year. Students of all ages are using my Foldables for daily work, note-taking activities, student-directed projects, as forms of alternative assessment, journals, graphs, charts, tables, and more. You may have seen at least one of the Foldables featured in this book used in supplemental programs or staff-development workshops.

After workshop presentations, participants would often ask me for lists of activities to be used with the Foldables they had just learned to make. They needed help visualizing how Foldables could be used to display the data associated with their disciplines—in this case, Elementary Science. So, over twenty-five years ago, I started collecting and sharing my ideas about how Foldables could be used to meet the needs of the science teacher.

This book is the fruit of those years. It is organized in three parts. The first part introduces Foldables, explaining how they work and some of the ways they can be used. The second part gives step-by-step instructions on how to make 34 basic Foldable activities, along with practical classroom-tested tips. Finally, the third part of the book presents suggestions for using Foldables with specific Science topics.

[signature]

Workshops

Contact Cecile Stepman
1-210-6980123
cecile@dinah.com

Orders

1-800-99DINAH
orders@dinah.com

E-Group

Join on website: www.dinah.com
or e-mail mindy@dinah.com

Why use Foldables in Science?

When teachers ask me why they should take time to use the Foldables featured in this book, I explain that they

. . . quickly organize, display, and arrange data, making it easier for students to grasp science concepts, theories, facts, opinions, questions, research, and ideas. They also help sequence events as outlined in the content standards.

. . . result in student-made study guides that are compiled as students listen for main ideas, read for main ideas, or conduct research.

. . . provide a multitude of creative formats in which students can present projects, research, interviews, and inquiry-based reports instead of typical poster board or science fair formats.

. . . replace teacher-generated writing or photocopied sheets with student-generated print.

. . . incorporate the use of such skills as comparing and contrasting, recognizing cause and effect, and finding similarities and differences into daily work and long-term projects. For example, these Foldables can be used to compare and contrast student explanations of inquiry-based questions to explanations currently accepted by scientists.

. . . continue to "immerse" students in previously learned vocabulary, concepts, information, generalizations, ideas, and theories, providing them with a strong foundation that they can build upon with new observations, concepts, and knowledge.

. . . can be used by students or teachers to easily communicate data through graphs, tables, charts, models, and diagrams, including Venn diagrams.

. . . allow students to make their own journals for recording qualitative and quantitative observations.

. . . can be used as alternative assessment tools by teachers to evaluate student progress or by students to evaluate their own progress.

. . . integrate language arts, social sciences, and mathematics into the study of science.

. . . provide a sense of student ownership or investment in the science curriculum.

National Science Standards and Communication Skills

The National Science Standards stress the importance of communication skills in science education. Not all students will become scientists, but all students need to be able to think, analyze, and communicate using in a scientific manner. Throughout their lives, students will be called upon to be science literate as they make observations, analyze and recall empirical data, read and differentiate between fact and opinion, discuss pros and cons of actions and reactions, justify voting for or against an issue, research a topic related to their well being or interests, make cause-and-effect decisions about their actions, write editorials to express their views publicly, and more. Foldables are one of many techniques that can be used to integrate reading, writing, thinking, debating, researching, and other communication skills into an interdisciplinary science curriculum.

Foldable Basics

What to Write and Where

Teach students to write general information--titles, vocabulary words, concepts, questions, main ideas, and laws or theorems--on the front tabs of their Foldables. General information is viewed every time a student looks at a Foldable. Foldables help students focus on and remember key points without being distracted by other print.

Ask students to write specific information—supporting ideas, student thoughts, answers to questions, research information, empirical data, class notes, observations, and definitions—under the tabs.

As you teach, demonstrate different ways in which Foldables can be used. Soon you will find that students make their own Foldables and use them independently for study guides and projects.

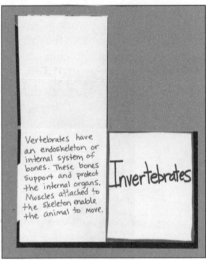

With or Without Tabs

Foldables with flaps or tabs create study guides that students can use to self check what they know about the general information on the front of tabs. Use Foldables without tabs for assessment purposes (where it's too late to self check) or projects where information is presented for others to view quickly.

Venn Diagram used as a study guide

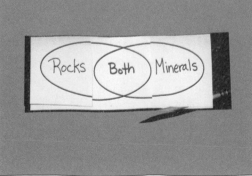

Venn Diagram used for assessment

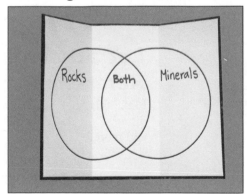

What to Do with Scissors and Glue

If it is difficult for your students to keep glue and scissors at their desks or to carry it from class to class, set up a small table in the classroom and provide several containers of glue, numerous pairs of scissors (sometimes tied to the table), containers of crayons or colored pencils, a stapler, clear tape, and anything else you think students might need to make their Foldables. Don't be surprised if students donate colored markers, decorative-edged scissors, gel pens, stencils, and other art items to your publishing table.

The more they make and use graphic organizers, the faster students become at producing them.

Storing Graphic Organizers in Student Portfolios

Turn one-gallon freezer bags into student portfolios which can be collected and stored in the classroom. Students can also carry their portfolios in their notebooks if they place strips of two-inch clear tape along one side and punch three holes through the taped edge.

Have each student write his or her name along the top of the plastic portfolio with a permanent marker and cover the writing with two-inch clear tape to keep it from wearing off.

Cut the bottom corners off the bag so it won't hold air and will stack and store easily.

HINT: *I found it more convenient to keep student portfolios in my classroom so student work was always available when needed and not "left at home" or "in the car." Giant laundry-soap boxes make good storage containers for portfolios.*

Let Students Use This Book As an Idea Reference

Make this book of lists available to students to use as an idea reference for projects, discussions, social studies debates, extra credit work, cooperative learning group presentations, and more.

Selecting the Appropriate Foldable

Dividing Science Concepts into Parts

Foldables divide information and make it visual. In order to select the appropriate Foldable, decide how many parts you want to divide the information into and then determine which Foldable best illustrates or fits those parts. Foldables that are three-dimensional also make the student interact with the data kinesthetically.

For example, If you are studying the three kinds of rocks, you could choose a Foldable that has three tabs (or sections), on the front tabs write *igneous*, *metamorphic*, and *sedimentary* and under the tabs, place information and examples of each type of rock.

Science Concepts Already Divided into Parts								
	Earth			*Life*			*Physical*	
Parts	**Concept**		**Parts**	**Concept**		**Parts**	**Concept**	
10	Moh's Scale		13	Vitamins		4	States of Matter	
4	Layers of Earth		2	Nocturnal and Diurnal		6	Simple Tools and Machines	
3	Eras of Geological Time		3	Monocots and Dicots		2	Kinetic and Potential Energy	
9	Solar System Planets		2	Vertebrates and Invertebrates		2	Convex and Concave Lenses	
5	Layers of the Atmosphere		6	Kingdoms of Living Organisms		3	Newton's Three Laws of Motion	
4	Reduce, Reuse, Recycle, Refuse		2	Living and Non-living		2	Sink and Float	
3	Igneous, Metamorphic, Sedimentary Rock		3	Producer, Consumer, Decomposer		3	Conduction, Convection, Radiation	

Science Concepts That Can Be Divided into Parts		
Earth	*Life*	*Statistics and Probability*
Air Pressure	A Life Cycle	Forces
Earth's Plates	Examples of Fungi	Types of Friction
Causes of Erosion	Parts of a Plant Cell	Properties of Magnetism
Formation of a Fossil	Human Digestive System	Physical Properties of Matter
Effects of Ocean Movement	Levels of Life in the Ocean	Radiant Energy
Weather Patterns over Time	Characteristics of Invertebrates	Examples of Inertia

Dividing Skills and Foldables into Parts

Reading, writing, and thinking skills can easily be used with Foldables. The following lists show examples of skills and activities and a selection of Foldables divided into parts. You may want to refer to this page as you select activities from the lists of Science topics in the third section of this book (see pages 43–115)

Skills and Activities Divided into Parts

1 Part	2 Parts
Find the Main Idea	Compare and Contrast
Predict an Outcome	Cause and Effect
Narrative Science Writing	Similarities and Differences
Descriptive Science Writing	Pros and Cons
Expository Science Writing	Facts and Opinions
Persuasive Science Writing	Form and Function
3 Parts	**4 Parts**
Venn Diagrams	Who, What, When, Where
Know?-Like to Know?-Learned?	What, Where, When, Why/How
Beginning, Middle, End	
Any Number of Parts	
Questioning	Making and Using Tables
Flow Charts	Making and Using Graphs
Vocabulary Words	Making and Using Charts
Time Lines	Sequencing Data or Events
Concept Webs or Maps	

Foldables Divided into Parts

1 Part	2 Parts
Half Book	Two-Tab Book
Folded Book	Pocket Book
Three-Quarter Book	Shutterfold
Picture-Frame Book	Matchbook Cut in Half
Bound Book	Forward-Backward Book
Matchbook	Concept Map with Two Tabs
3 Parts	**4 Parts**
Trifold Book	Four-Tab Book
Three-Tab Book	Standing Cube
Pyramid Book	Top-Tab Book
Three Pocket Book	Four-Door Book
Concept Map with Three Tabs	
Any Number of Parts	
Accordion Book	Circle Graph
Layered-Look Book	Concept-Map Book
Sentence-Strip Holder	Vocabulary Book
Sentence Strips	Pyramid Mobile
Bound Book	Pop-Up Book
Top-Tab Book (three or more sheets of paper)	Multiple-Pocket Books
Billboard Project	Project Board with Tabs
Display Case	Folded Table, Chart, or Graph

Basic Foldable Shapes

The following figures illustrate the basic folds that are referred to throughout the following section of this book

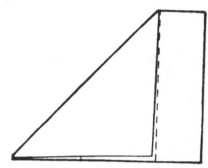

Taco Fold

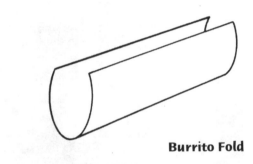

Hamburger Fold

Hot Dog Fold

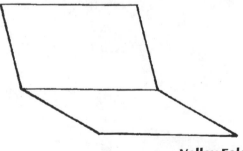

Burrito Fold

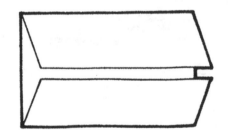

Shutter Fold

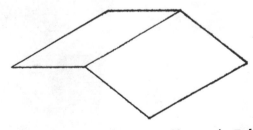

Valley Fold

Mountain Fold

Half-Book

Fold a sheet of paper (8 1/2" χ 11") in half.

1. This book can be folded vertically like a *hot dog* or . . .

2. . . . it can be folded horizontally like a *hamburger.*

Use this book for descriptive, expository, persuasive, or narrative writing, as well as graphs, diagrams, or charts.

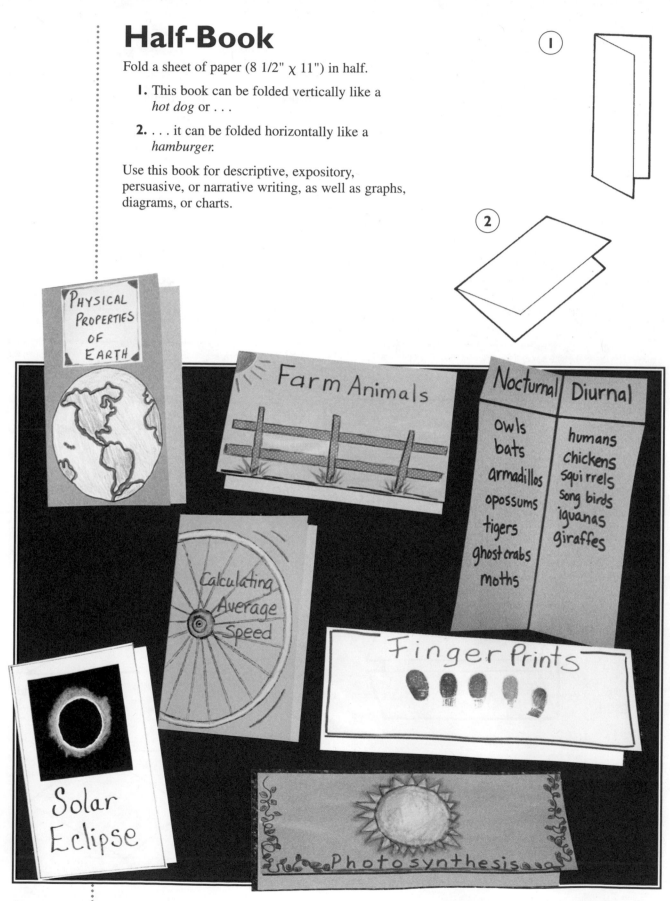

Folded Book

1. Make a *half-book*.

2. Fold it in half again like a *hamburger*. This makes a ready-made cover, and two small pages for information on the inside.

Use photocopied work sheets, Internet print outs, and student-drawn diagrams or maps to make this book. One sheet of paper becomes two activities and two grades.

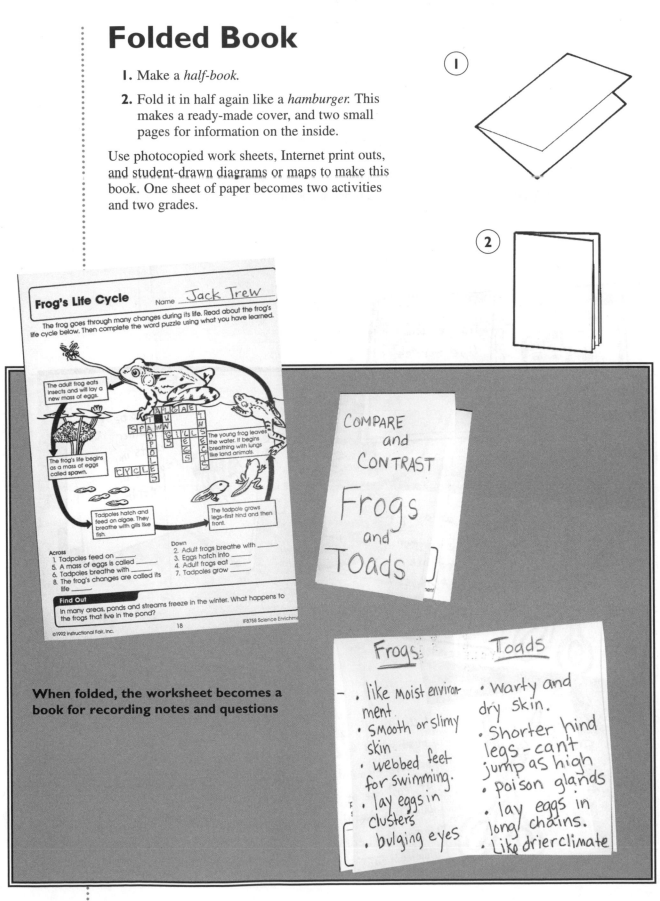

When folded, the worksheet becomes a book for recording notes and questions

Three-Quarter Book

1. Take a *two-tab* book and raise the left-hand tab.

2. Cut the tab off at the top fold line.

3. A larger book of information can be made by gluing several *three-quarter books* side-by-side.

Sketch or glue a graphic to the left, write one or more questions on the right, and record answers and information under the right tab.

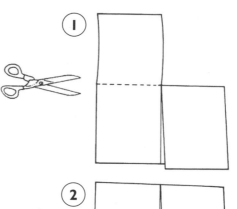

Bound Book

1. Take two sheets of paper (8 1/2" χ 11") and separately fold them like a *hamburger*. Place the papers on top of each other, leaving one sixteenth of an inch between the *mountain tops*.

2. Mark both folds one inch from the outer edges.

3. On one of the folded sheets, cut from the top and bottom edge to the marked spot on both sides.

4. On the second folded sheet, start at one of the marked spots and cut the fold between the two marks.

5. Take the cut sheet from step 3 and fold it like a *burrito*. Place the *burrito* through the other sheet and then open the *burrito*. Fold the bound pages in half to form an eight-page book.

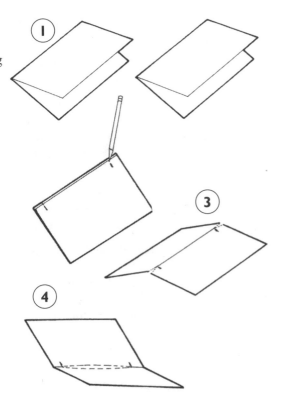

Picture-Frame Book

1. Fold a sheet of paper (8 1/2" χ 11") in half like a *hamburger*.

2. Open the *hamburger* and gently roll one side of the *hamburger* toward the *valley*. Try not to crease the roll.

3. Cut a rectangle out of the middle of the rolled side of the paper leaving a half-inch border, forming a frame.

4. Fold another sheet of paper (8 1/2" χ 11") in half like a *hamburger*. Apply glue to the inside border of the picture frame and place the folded, uncut sheet of paper inside.

Use this book to feature a person, place, or thing. Inside the picture frames, glue photographs, magazine pictures, computer-generated graphs, or have students sketch pictures. This book has three inside pages for writing and recording notes.

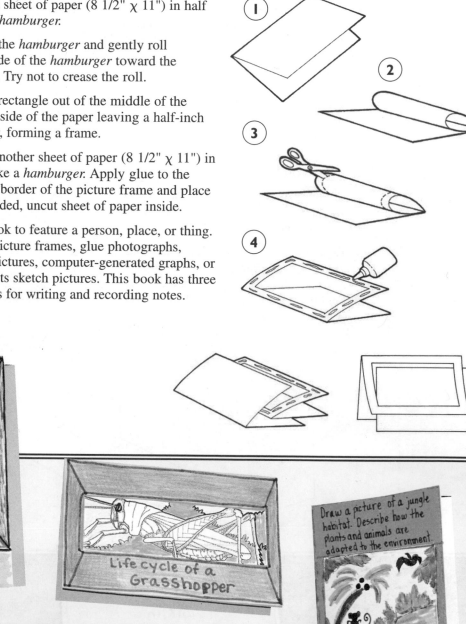

Two-Tab Book

1. Take a *folded book* and cut up the *valley* of the inside fold toward the *mountain top*. This cut forms two large tabs that can be used front and back for writing and illustrations.

2. The book can be expanded by making several of these folds and gluing them side-by-side.

Use this book with data occurring in twos. For example, use it for comparing and contrasting, determining cause and effect, finding similarities and differences, and more.

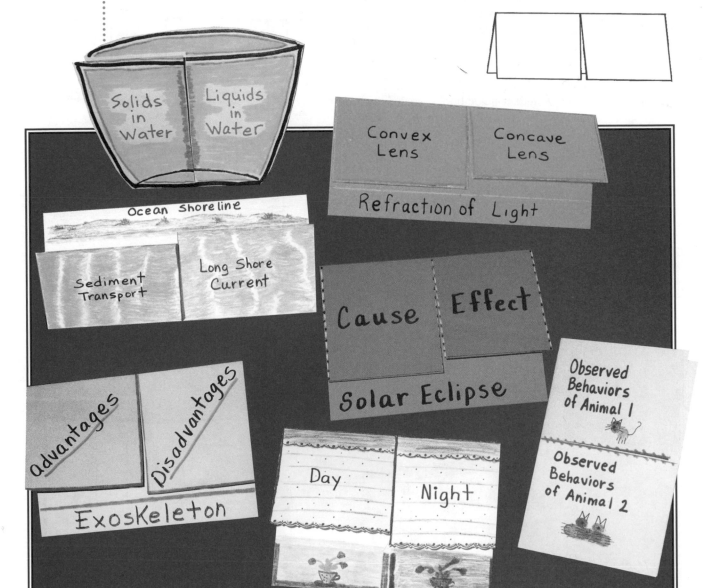

Pocket Book

1. Fold a sheet of paper (8 1/2" χ 11") in half like a *hamburger*.

2. Open the folded paper and fold one of the long sides up two inches to form a pocket. Refold along the *hamburger* fold so that the newly formed pockets are on the inside.

3. Glue the outer edges of the two-inch fold with a small amount of glue.

4. Optional: Glue a cover around the *pocket book.*

Variation: Make a multi-paged booklet by gluing several pockets side-by-side. Glue a cover around the multi-paged *pocket book.*

Use 3" χ 5" index cards and quarter-sheets of notebook paper inside the pockets. Store student-made books, such as two-tab books and folded books in the pockets.

Matchbook

1. Fold a sheet of paper (8 1/2" χ 11") like a *hamburger,* but fold it so that one side is one inch longer than the other side.

2. Fold the one-inch tab over the short side forming an envelopelike fold.

3. Cut the front flap in half toward the *mountain top* to create two flaps.

Use this book to report on one thing, such as one person, place, or thing, or for reporting on two things, such as the cause and effect of water pollution.

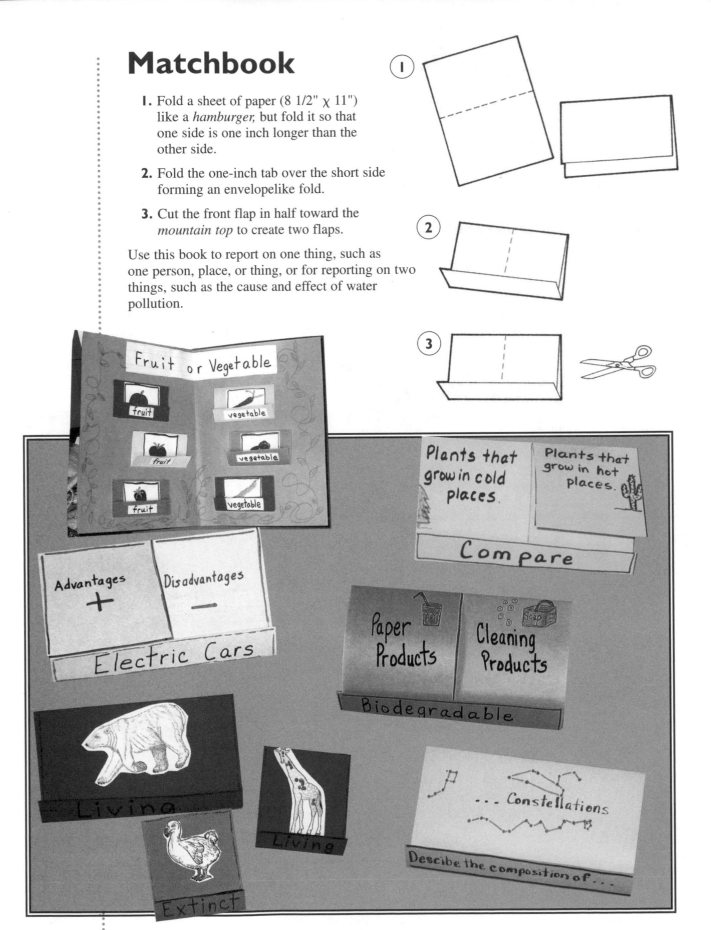

Shutter Fold

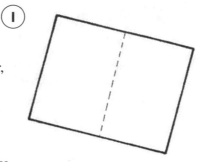

1. Begin as if you were going to make a *hamburger* but instead of creasing the paper, pinch it to show the midpoint.

2. Fold the outer edges of the paper to meet at the pinch, or mid-point, forming a *shutter fold.*

Use this book for data occurring in twos. Or, make this fold using 11" χ 17" paper and smaller books—such as the half book, journal, and two-tab book—that can be glued inside to create a large project full of student work.

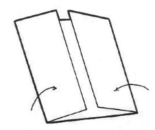

Forward-Backward Book

1. Stack three or more sheets of paper. On the top sheet trace a large circle.

2. With the papers still stacked, cut out the circles.

3. Staple the paper circles together along the left-hand side to create a book.

4. Label the cover and takes notes on the pages that open to the right.

5. Turn the book upside down and label the back. Takes notes on the pages that open to the right.

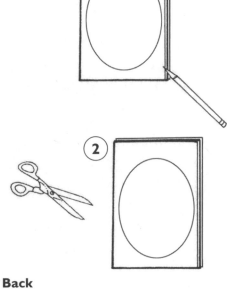

Front

Back

Front

Back

Use one Forward-Backward book to compare and contrast two people, places, things, or events.

Three-Tab Book

1. Fold a sheet of paper like a *hot dog*.

2. With the paper horizontal, and the fold of the *hot dog* up, fold the right side toward the center, trying to cover one half of the paper.

NOTE: *If you fold the right edge over first, the final graphic organizer will open and close like a book.*

3. Fold the left side over the right side to make a book with three folds.

4. Open the folded book. Place your hands between the two thicknesses of paper and cut up the two *valleys* on one side only. This will form three tabs.

Use this book for data occurring in threes, and for two-part Venn diagrams.

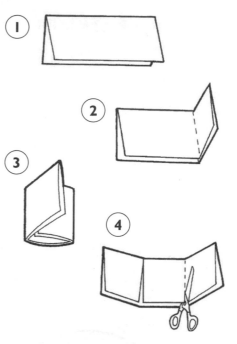

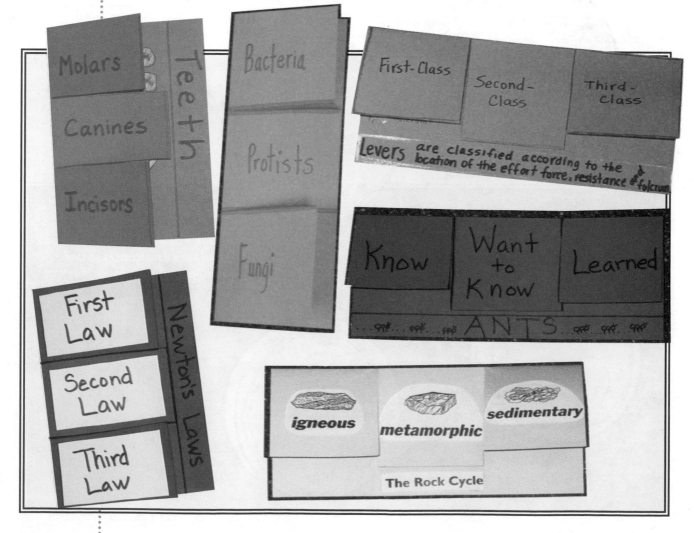

Three-Tab Book Variations

VARIATION A:
Draw overlapping circles on the three tabs
to make a Venn Diagram

VARIATION B:
Cut each of the three tabs in half to make
a six-tab book.

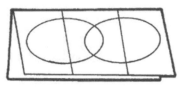

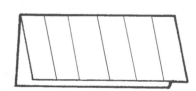

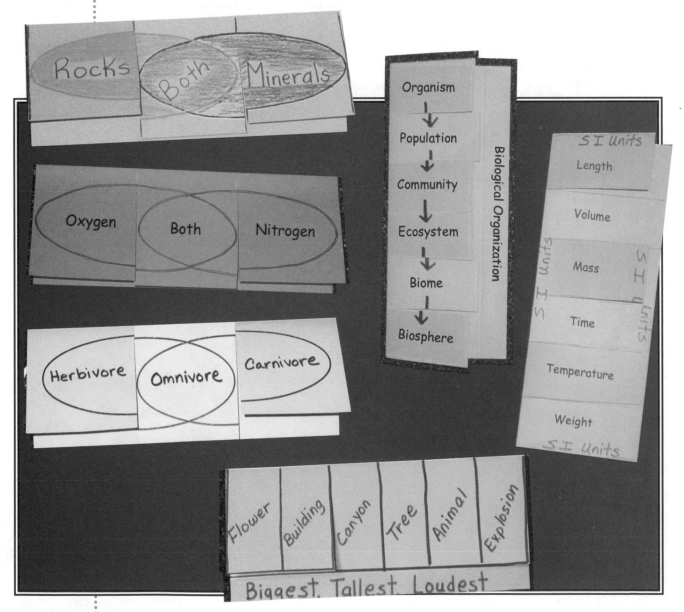

Pyramid Fold

1. Fold a sheet of paper (8 1/2" χ 11") into a *taco*, forming a square. Cut off the excess rectangular tab formed by the fold.

2. Open the folded *taco* and refold it the opposite way forming another *taco* and an X-fold pattern.

3. Cut one of the folds to the center of the X, or the midpoint, and stop. This forms two triangular-shaped flaps.

4. Glue one of the flaps under the other, forming a *pyramid*.

5. Label front sections and write information, notes, thoughts, and questions inside the pyramid on the back of the appropriate tab.

**Use to make mobiles and dioramas.
Use with data occurring in threes.**

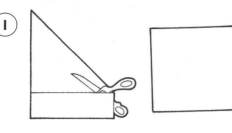

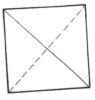
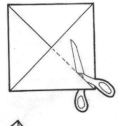
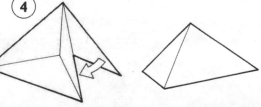
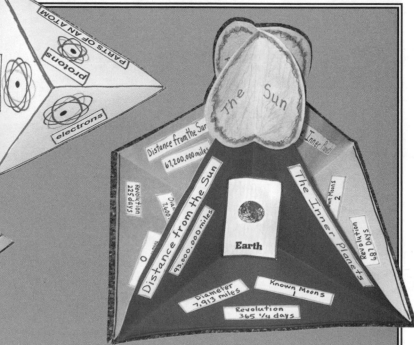

Trifold Book

1. Fold a sheet of paper (8 1/2" χ 11") into thirds.

2. Use this book as is, or cut into shapes. If the trifold is cut, leave plenty of fold on both sides of the designed shape, so the book will open and close in three sections.

Use this book to make charts with three columns or rows, large Venn diagrams, reports on data occurring in threes, or to show the outside and inside of something and to write about it.

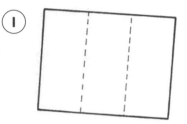

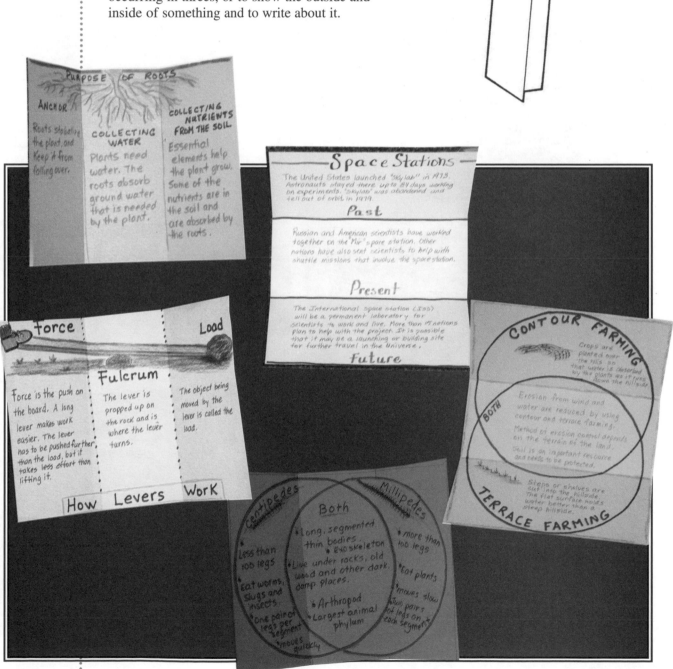

Three Pocket Book

1. Fold a horizontal sheet of paper (11" χ 17") into thirds.

2. Fold the bottom edge up two inches and crease well. Glue the outer edges of the two inch tab to create three pockets.

3. Label each pocket. Use to hold notes taken on index cards or quarter sheets of paper.

①

②

③

Earthquake Safety Tips

| Know which radio station to use for emergency | At home, go in the corner of the room away from windows | Stay out of buildings that are |
| Before | During | After |

Life Forms:

| Plants: Conifers and terrestrial plants appear | Jurassic: First modern birds appear | Life Forms: Mammals and modern marine animals increase in number |

PALEOZOIC ERA

MESOZOIC ERA
(AGE OF DINOSAURS)

CENOZOIC ERA
(AGE OF MAMMALS)

| Metals conduct electricity | Poor conductors of heat | Used to make chips |
| Metals | Nonmetals | Metalloids |

Fungi   Vocabulary

| Club fungi most mushrooms have gills hold spores | Mycorrhiza: an irritation formed at roots of plants or a fungi | Lichen: formed when a fungi and either a bacteria or a cyano live together |
| Know | Need to Know | Learned |

Major Ecosystems

| Forests, deserts, prairies and meadows are terrestrial | freshwater eco-systems include lakes, ponds and streams. | Saltwater ecosystems make up almost 75% of the |
| Terrestrial | Freshwater | Saltwater |

Four-Tab Book

1. Fold a sheet of paper (8 1/2" χ 11") in half like a *hot dog*.

2. Fold this long rectangle in half like a *hamburger*.

3. Fold both ends back to touch the *mountain top* or fold it like an *accordion*.

4. On the side with two *valleys* and one *mountain top*, make vertical cuts through one thickness of paper, forming four tabs.

Use this book for data occurring in fours. For example: skin, nails, hair, and teeth.

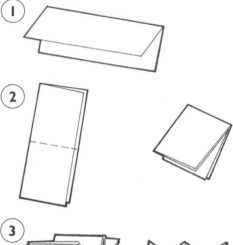

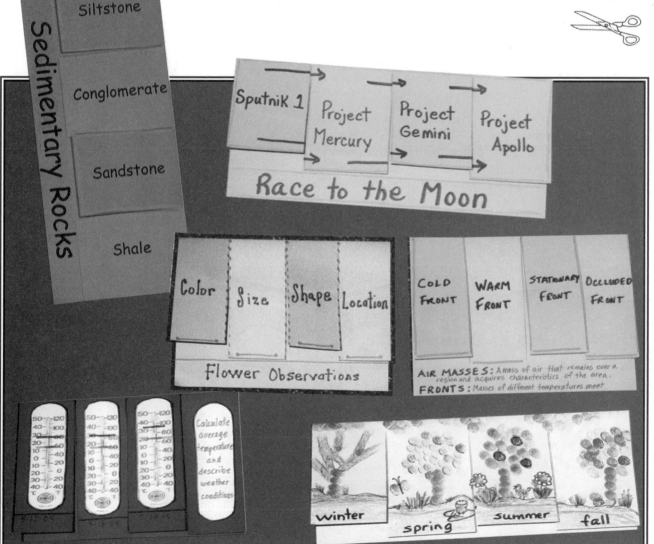

Standing Cube

1. Use two sheets of the same size paper. Fold each like a *hamburger*. However, fold one side one half inch shorter than the other side. This will make a tab that extends out one half inch on one side.

2. Fold the long side over the short side of both sheets of paper, making tabs.

3. On one of the folded papers, place a small amount of glue along the the small folded tab, next to the *valley* but not in it.

4. Place the non-folded edge of the second sheet of paper square into the *valley* and fold the glue-covered tab over this sheet of paper. Press flat until the glue holds. Repeat with the other side.

5. Allow the glue to dry completely before continuing. After the glue has dried, the cube can be collapsed flat to allow students to work at their desks. The cube can also be folded into fourths for easier storage, or for moving it to a display area.

Use with data occurring in fours or make it into a project. Make a small display cube using 8 1/2" χ 11" paper. Use 11" χ 17" paper to make large project cubes that you can glue other books onto for display. Notebook paper, photocopied sheets, magazine pictures, and current events also can be displayed on the large cube.

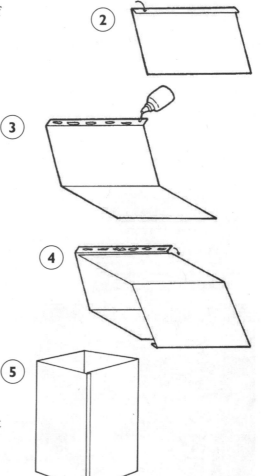

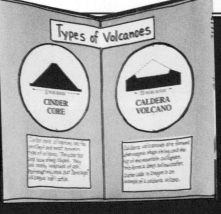

This large cube project can be folded and stored in plastic bag portfolios.

Four-Door Book

1. Make a *shutter fold* using 11" χ 17" or 12" χ 18" paper.

2. Fold the *shutter fold* in half like a *hamburger.* Crease well.

3. Open the project and cut along the two inside *valley* folds.

4. These cuts will form four doors on the inside of the project.

Use this fold for data occurring in fours. When folded in half like a *hamburger,* a finished *four-door book* can be glued inside a large (11" χ 17") *shutter fold* as part of a larger project.

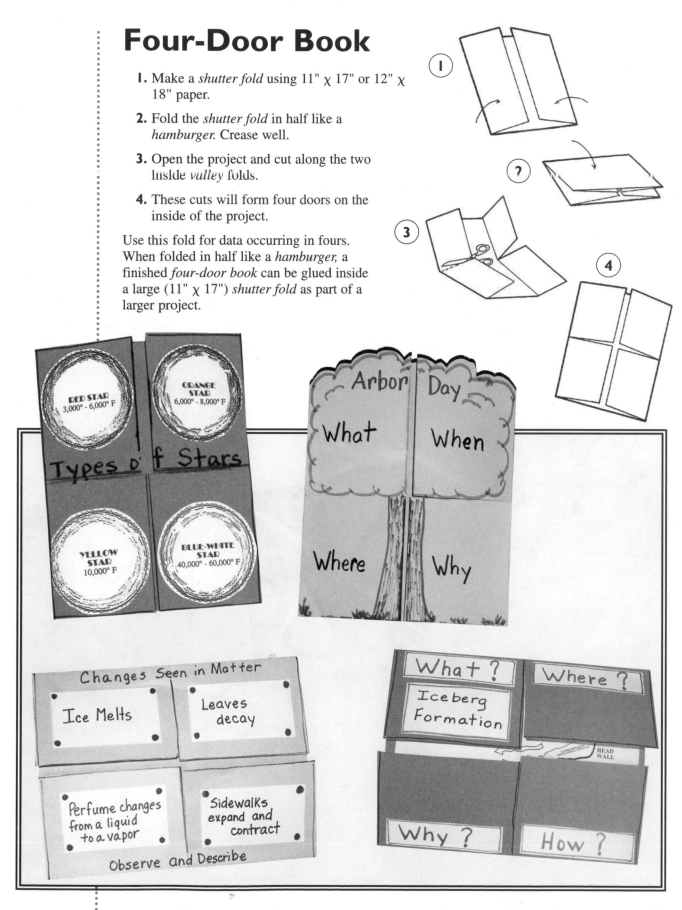

23

Envelope Fold

1. Fold a sheet of paper (8 1/2" χ 11") into a taco forming a square. Cut off the excess paper strip formed by the square.

2. Open the folded taco and refold it the opposite way forming another taco and an X fold pattern.

3. Open the taco fold and fold the corners toward the center point of the X forming a small square.

4. Trace this square on another sheet of paper. Cut and glue it to the inside of the envelope. Pictures can be placed under or on top of the tabs, or can be used to teach fractional parts.

Use this book for data occurring in fours. For example: infancy, childhood, adolescence, and adulthood

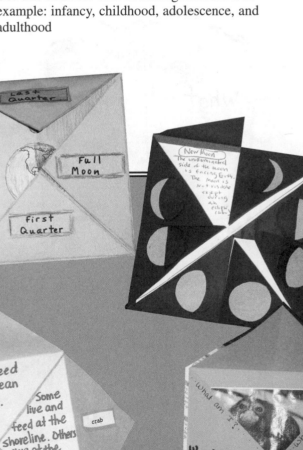

Layered-Look Book

1. Stack two sheets of paper (8 1/2" χ 11") so that the back sheet is one inch higher than the front sheet.

2. Bring the bottom of both sheets upward and align the edges so that all of the layers or tabs are the same distance apart.

3. When all tabs are an equal distance apart, fold the papers and crease well.

4. Open the papers and glue them together along the *valley* or inner center fold or, staple them along the mountain.

MOST COMMON ELEMENTS IN THE EARTH'S CRUST	
Iron (Fe)	.34%
Silicon (Si)	.88%
Oxygen (O)	94%
Calcium (Ca)	1%
Magnesium (Mg)	.26%

queen

drone

worker

BEE COLONY

SIMPLE MACHINES

SCREW

PULLEY

WEDGE

LEVER

WHEEL AND AXLE

INCLINED PLANE

My Invention

ROCK MOVEMENT

FAULT LINE

SIDEWAYS MOVEMENT

UPWARD MOVEMENT

DOWNWARD MOVEMENT

Predictions of Future Movement

MOLECULES

MIXTURES

COMPOUNDS

ELEMENTS

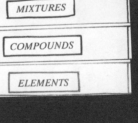

SUN

Mercury

Venus

Earth

Mars

Jupiter

Saturn

Uranus

Neptune

Pluto

surface dwellers

free swimmers

bottom dwellers

LIFE IN THE OCEAN

When using more than two sheets of paper, make the tabs smaller than an inch.

Top-Tab Book

1. Fold a sheet of paper (8 1/2" χ 11") in half like a *hamburger*. Cut the center fold, forming two half sheets.

2. Fold one of the half sheets four times. Begin by folding in half like a *hamburger,* fold again like a *hamburger,* and finally again like a *hamburger.* This folding has formed your pattern of four rows and four columns, or 16 small squares.

3. Fold two sheets of paper (8 1/2" χ 11") in half like a *hamburger*. Cut the center folds, forming four half sheets.

4. Hold the pattern vertically and place on a half sheet of paper under the pattern. Cut the bottom right hand square out of both sheets. Set this first page aside.

5. Take a second half sheet of paper and place it under the pattern. Cut the first and second right hand squares out of both sheets. Place the second page on top of the first page.

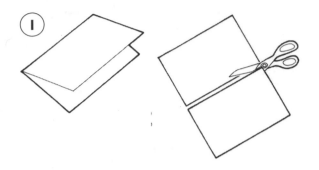

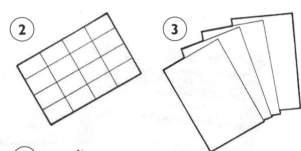

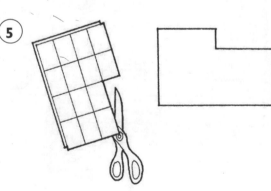

6. Take a third half sheet of paper and place it under the pattern. Cut the first, second, and third right hand squares out of both sheets. Place this third page on top of the second page.

7. Place the fourth, uncut half sheet of paper behind the three cut out sheets, leaving four aligned tabs across the top of the book. Staple several times on the left side. You can also place glue along the left paper edges, and stack them together. The glued spine is very strong.

8. Cut a final half sheet of paper with no tabs and staple along the left side to form a cover.

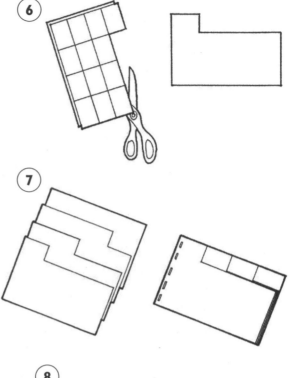

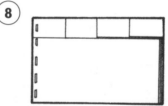

Accordion Book

NOTE: *Steps 1 and 2 should be done only if paper is too large to begin with.*

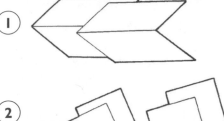

1. Fold the selected paper into *hamburgers*.

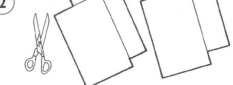

2. Cut the paper in half along the fold lines.

3. Fold each section of paper into *hamburgers*. However, fold one side one half inch shorter than the other side. This will form a tab that is one half inch long.

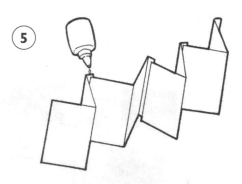

4. Fold this tab forward over the shorter side, and then fold it back away from the shorter piece of paper (in other words, fold it the opposite way).

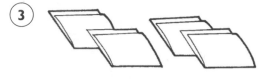

5. Glue together to form an *accordion* by gluing a straight edge of one section into the *valley* of another section.

NOTE: *Stand the sections on end to form an accordion to help students visualize how to glue them together. (See illustration.)*

Always place the extra tab at the back of the book so you can add more pages later.

Use this book for timelines, student projects that grow, sequencing events or data, and biographies.

When folded, this project is used like a book, and it can be stored in student portfolios. When open, it makes a nice project display. Accordion books can be stored in file cabinets

Pop-Up Book

1. Fold a sheet of paper (8 1/2" χ 11") in half like a *hamburger*.

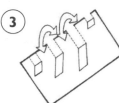

2. Beginning at the fold, or *mountain* top, cut one or more tabs.

3. Fold the tabs back and forth several times until there is a good fold line formed.

4. Partially open the *hamburger* fold and push the tabs through to the inside.

5. With one small dot of glue, glue figures for the *pop-up book* to the front of each tab. Allow the glue to dry before going on to the next step.

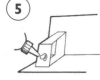

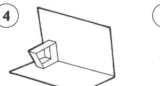

6. Make a cover for the book by folding another sheet of paper in half like a *hamburger*. Place glue around the outside edges of the *pop-up book* and firmly press inside the *hamburger* cover.

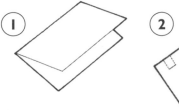

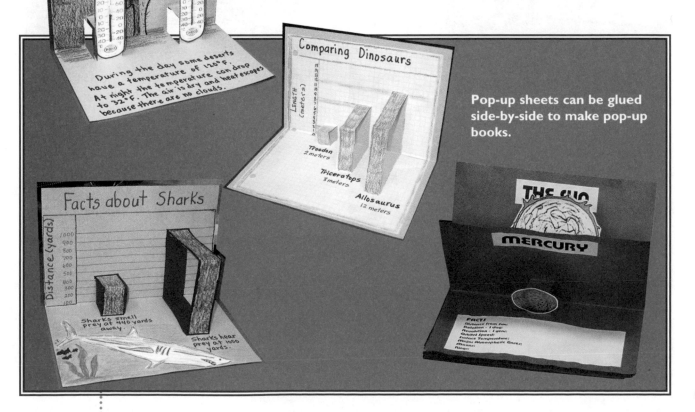

Pop-up sheets can be glued side-by-side to make pop-up books.

Folding into fifths

1. Fold a sheet of paper in half like a hotdog or hamburger for a five tab book, or leave open for a folded table or chart.

2. Fold the paper so that one third is exposed and two thirds are covered.

3. Fold the two thirds section in half.

4.Fold the one third section (single thickness) backward to form a fold line.

The paper will be divided into fifths when opened

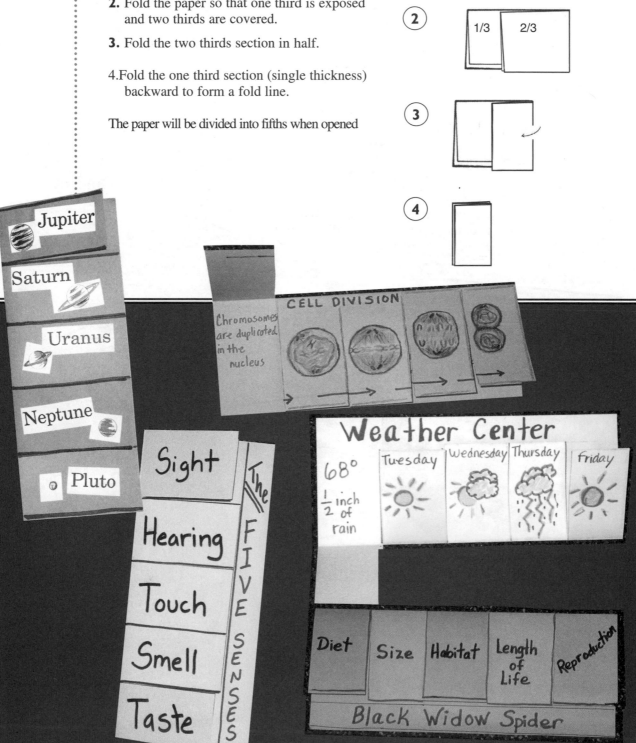

Folded Table or Chart

1. Fold the number of vertical columns needed to make the table or chart.

2. Fold the horizontal rows needed to make the table or chart.

3. Label the rows and columns.

Remember: Tables are organized along vertical and horizontal axes, while charts are organized along one axis, either horizontal or vertical.

Table

Chart

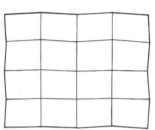

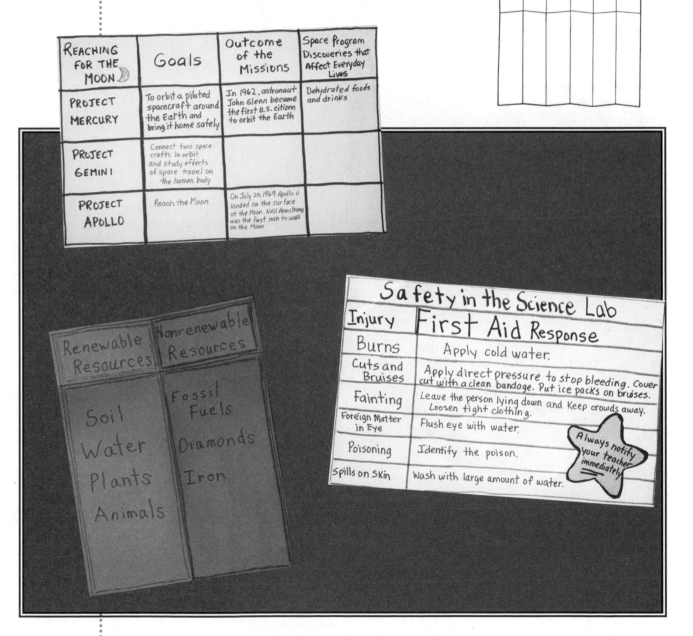

REACHING FOR THE MOON ☽	Goals	Outcome of the Missions	Space Program Discoveries that Affect Everyday Lives
PROJECT MERCURY	To orbit a piloted spacecraft around the Earth and bring it home safely	In 1962, astronaut John Glenn became the first U.S. citizen to orbit the Earth	Dehydrated foods and drinks
PROJECT GEMINI	Connect two spacecrafts in orbit and study effects of space travel on the human body		
PROJECT APOLLO	Reach the Moon	On July 20, 1969 Apollo 11 landed on the surface of the Moon. Neil Armstrong was the first man to walk on the Moon	

Renewable Resources	Nonrenewable Resources
Soil Water Plants Animals	Fossil Fuels Diamonds Iron

Safety in the Science Lab

Injury	First Aid Response
Burns	Apply cold water.
Cuts and Bruises	Apply direct pressure to stop bleeding. Cover cut with a clean bandage. Put ice packs on bruises.
Fainting	Leave the person lying down and keep crowds away. Loosen tight clothing.
Foreign Matter in Eye	Flush eye with water.
Poisoning	Identify the poison.
Spills on Skin	Wash with large amount of water.

Always notify your teacher immediately

Folding a Circle into Tenths

1. Fold a paper circle in half.

2. Fold the half circle so that one third is exposed and two thirds are covered.

3. Fold the one third (single thickness) backward to form a fold line.

4. Fold the two thirds section in half.

5. The half circle will be divided into fifths. When opened, the circle will be divided into tenths.

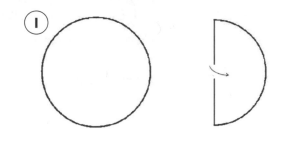

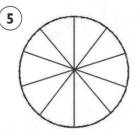

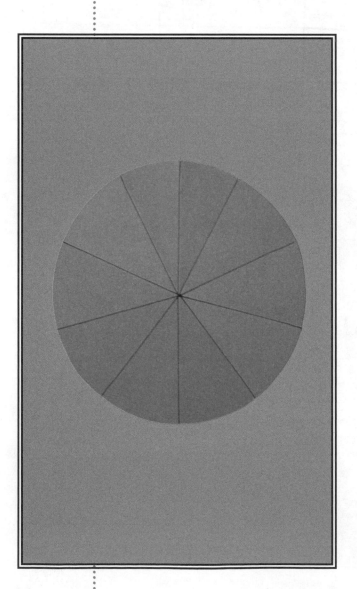

NOTE: *Paper squares and rectangles are folded into tenths the same way. Fold them so that one third is exposed and two thirds is covered. Continue with steps 3 and 4.*

Circle Graph

1. Cut out two circles using a pattern.

2. Fold one of the circles in half on each axis, forming fourths. Cut along one of the fold lines (the radius) to the middle of each circle. Flatten the circle.

3. Slip the two circles together along the cuts until they overlap completely.

4. Spin one of the circles while holding the other stationary. Estimate how much of each of the two (or you can add more) circles should be exposed to illustrate given percentages or fractional parts of data. Add circles to represent more than two percentages.

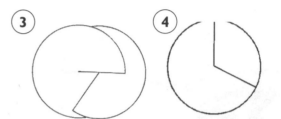

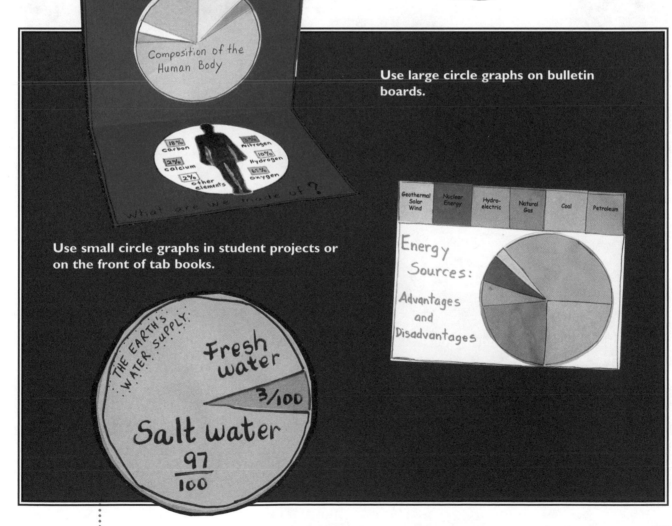

Use large circle graphs on bulletin boards.

Use small circle graphs in student projects or on the front of tab books.

Vocabulary Book

1. Fold a sheet of notebook paper in half like a *hotdog*.

2. On one side, cut every third line. This results in ten tabs on wide ruled notebook paper and twelve tabs on college ruled.

3. Label the tabs.

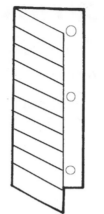

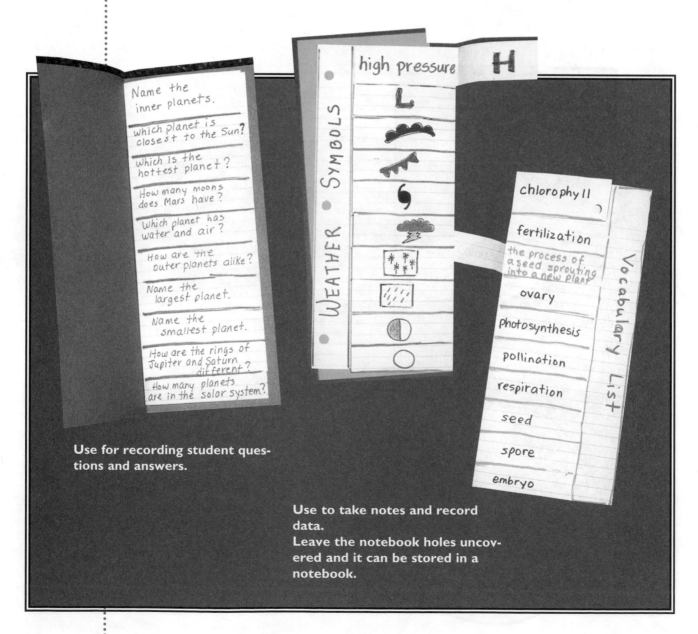

Use for recording student questions and answers.

Use to take notes and record data.
Leave the notebook holes uncovered and it can be stored in a notebook.

Concept-Map Book

1. Fold a sheet of paper along the long or short axis, leaving a two-inch tab uncovered along the top.

2. Fold in half or in thirds.

3. Unfold and cut along the two or three inside fold lines.

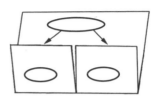

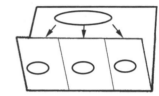

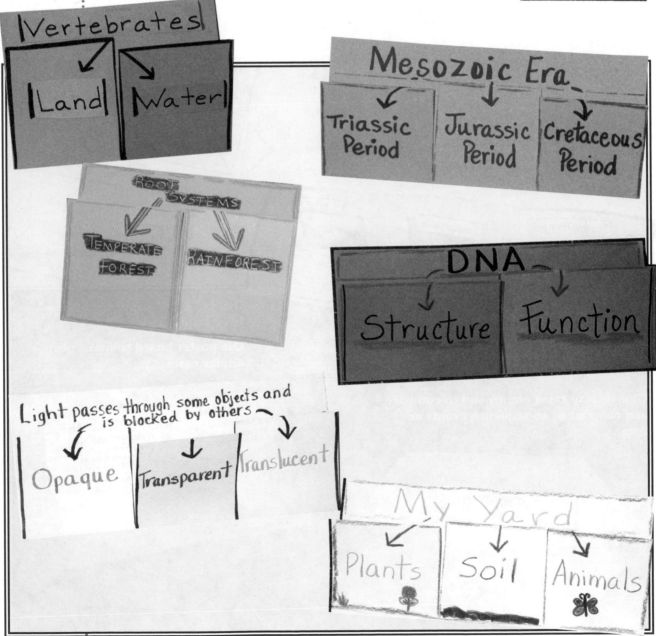

Four-Door Diorama

1. Make a *four-door book* out of a *shutter fold.*

2. Fold the two inside corners back to the outer edges (*mountains*) of the *shutter fold.* This will result in two *tacos* that will make the *four-door book* look like it has a shirt collar. Do the same thing to the bottom of the *four-door book.* When finished, four small triangular *tacos* have been made.

3. Form a 90-degree angle and overlap the folded triangles to make a display case that doesn't use staples or glue. (It can be collapsed for storage.)

4. Or, as illustrated, cut off all four triangles, or *tacos.* Staple or glue the sides.

Use 11" x 17" paper to make a large display case.

Use poster board to make giant display cases.

Glue display cases end-to-end to compare and contrast or to sequence events or data.

Display Case

1. Make a *taco* fold and cut off the rectangular tab formed. This will result in a square.

2. Fold the square into a *shutter fold.*

3. Unfold and fold the square into another *shutter fold* perpendicular to the direction of the first. This will form a small square at each of the four corners of the sheet of paper.

4. As illustrated, cut along two fold lines on opposite sides of the large square.

5. Collapse in and glue the cut tabs to form an open box.

How to Make a Lid

Fold another open-sided box using a square of paper one half inch larger than the square used to make the first box. This will make a lid that fits snugly over the display box. *Example:* If the base is made out of an 8 1/2" paper square, then make the top out of a 9" square.

Cut a hole out of the lid and cover the opening with a cut piece of acetate used on overhead projectors. Heavy, clear plastic wrap or scraps from a laminating machine also will work. Secure the clear plastic sheet to the inside of the lid with glue or tape.

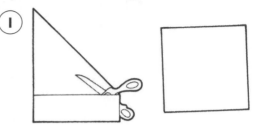

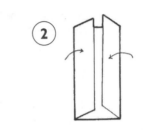

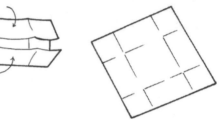

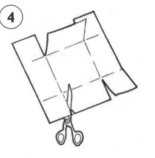

Project Board with Tabs

1. Draw a large illustration or a series of small illustrations or write on the front of one of the pieces of selected-size paper.

2. Pinch and slightly fold the paper at the point where a tab is desired on the illustrated project board. Cut into the paper on the fold. Cut straight in, then cut up to form an "L." When the paper is unfolded, it will form a tab with an illustration on the front.

3. After all tabs have been cut, glue this front sheet onto a second piece of paper. Place glue around all four edges and in the middle, away from tabs.

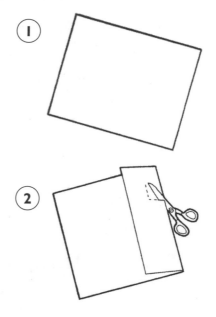

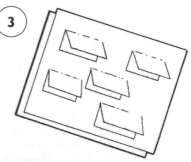

Killer whales can swim 30 mph. They are predators but do not harm humans. They surface to breathe air.

They do not have gills. They come to the surface to get oxygen.

are very large and may weigh 500 pounds

Vertebrates in the Ocean

Eels have snake-like shapes and fit in tight spaces.

Students write or draw under the tabs. If the project is made as a bulletin board using butcher paper, quarter and half-sheets of paper can be glued under the tabs.

Billboard Project

1. Fold all pieces of the same size of paper in half like *hamburgers*.

2. Place a line of glue at the top and bottom of one side of each folded billboard section and glue them edge-to-edge on a background paper or project board. If glued correctly, all doors will open from right to left.

3. Pictures, dates, words, etc., go on the front of each billboard section. When opened, writing or drawings can be seen on the inside left of each section. The base, or the part glued to the background, is perfect for more in-depth information or definitions.

Use for timelines or sequencing data, such as the stages of pregnancy or the path of the digestive system.

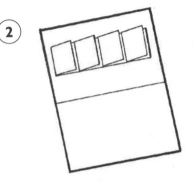

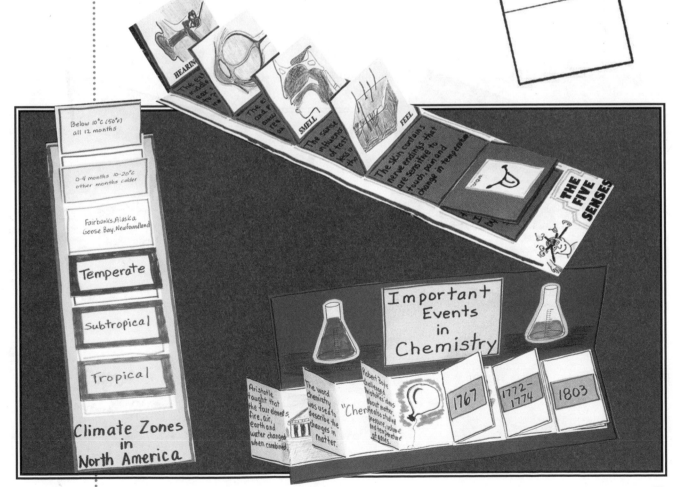

Sentence Strips

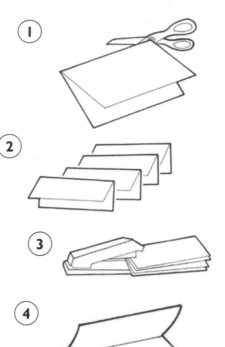

1. Take two sheets of paper (8 1/2" x 11") and fold into hamburgers. Cut along the fold lines making four half sheets. *(Use as many half sheets as necessary for additional pages to your book.)*

2. Fold each sheet in half like a hotdog.

3. Place the folds side-by-side and staple them together on the left side.

4. 1" from the stapled edge, cut the front page of each folded section up to the mountain top. These cuts form flaps that can be raised and lowered.

To make a half-cover, use a sheet of construction paper one inch longer than the book. Glue the back of the last sheet to the construction paper strip leaving one inch, on the left side, to fold over and cover the original staples. Staple this half-cover in place.

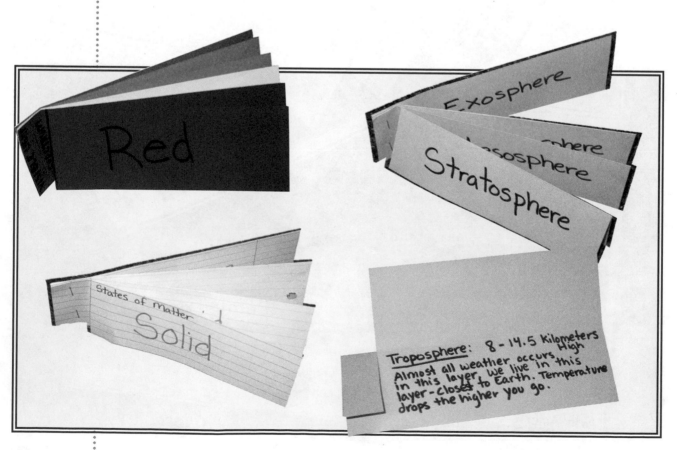

Sentence-Strip Holder

1. Fold a sheet of paper (8 1/2" χ 11") in half like a *hamburger*.

2. Open the *hamburger* and fold the two outer edges toward the *valley*. This forms a *shutter fold*.

3. Fold one of the inside edges of the shutter back to the outside fold. This fold forms a floppy "L."

4. Glue the floppy L-tab down to the base so that it forms a strong, straight L-tab.

5. Glue the other shutter side to the front of this L-tab. This forms a tent that is the backboard for the flashcards or student work to be displayed.

6. Fold the edge of the L-tab up one quarter to one half to form a lip that will keep the student work from slipping off the holder.

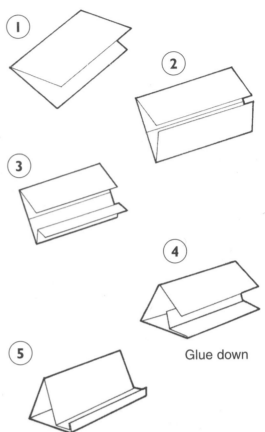

Glue down

Use holders to display student work on a table, or glue onto a bulletin board to make it interactive.

General Topics

The following Science topics are covered in this section.

General Topics

The following Science topics are covered in this section.

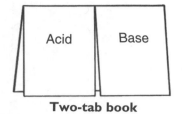

Acid | Base

Two-tab book

Acids and Bases

Skill	Activity Suggestion	Foldable Parts
question	create a "know?-like to know? -learned" about acids and bases	3
define	acid, base, neutral	3
chart	foods as acid, base, or neutral • acid: orange, lemon, vinegar, others • base: milk, • neutral: water	3
find	three common household items that are bases	3
	three common household items that are acids	3
diagram	a color-coded pH scale; 0-14	any number
explain	two ways to neutralize acid	2
	how vinegar cleans water spots off glass	1
observe	what happens to a chicken bone in vinegar	1
graph	pH levels of 3 different foods	3
research	how to treat insect stings that are acidic and those that are base	2
describe	tooth decay as it relates to acids and bases	2

Three-tab Venn diagram

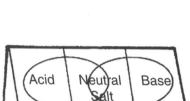

N | O

Two-tab book

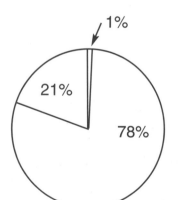

Air

Skill	Activity Suggestion	Foldable Parts
question	create a "know?-like to know? -learned" about air	3
inhale	describe what you feel and explain how the air takes up space in your body	2
explain	the importance of air to plants and animals	2
identify	on a periodic table of elements the two most common elements (gases) that form air	2
list	three common gases from greatest to least	3
graph	the percentages of common gases: • nitrogen = 78% • oxygen = 21% • others = 1%	3
describe	four other things (particulates) that can be found in air: smoke, dust, pollen, pollutants, volcanic ash, others	4
show cause and effect	of high and low air pressure	2

 1%

21%

78%

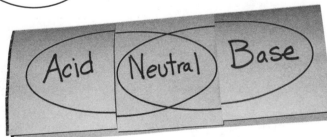

Algae

Skill	Activity Suggestion	Foldable Parts
question	create a "know?-like to know? -learned" about algae	3
describe	algae as living and explain its relationship to the Protist Kingdom	2
compare	the sizes of algae: microscopic, pond scum, sea weed	any number
show	algae as part of a four or more tiered energy pyramid *example:* algae, small fish, seal, killer whale	4+
explain	why plants and algae are called "producers"	2
	the importance of algae to living things	1
research	slime molds, diatoms, green algae, others	3+
determine	two things all algae have in common	2

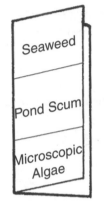

**Layered-look book
(2 sheets of paper)**

Amphibians

Skill	Activity Suggestion	Foldable Parts
question	create a "know?-like to know? -learned" about amphibians	3
describe	the relationship between amphibians and water	2
	the life of an amphibian in and out of water	2
chart	different kinds of amphibians, possibly including diet, size, color, habitat, and reproduction	any number
make a Venn diagram	comparing characteristics of toads and frogs	3
compare and contrast	amphibians with and without tails and/or legs	2
	the skin of an amphibian and a fish	2
	amphibian eggs and bird or reptile eggs	2
illustrate	the life cycle of a frog or toad, including egg, legless tadpole, tadpole with legs, young frog, adult	5
list	five characteristics of amphibians: • begin life in water • moist skin • four limbs • webbed feet • cold-blooded	5
research	three groups of amphibians: • frogs and toads • salamanders • caecilians	3

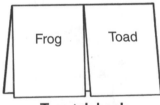

Three-tab book

Two-tab book

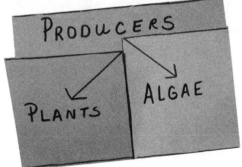

Angiosperms

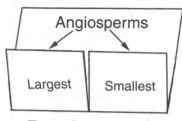

Two-tab concept map

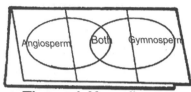

Three-tab Venn diagram

Skill	Activity Suggestion	Foldable Parts
question	create a "know?-like to know? -learned" about angiosperms	3
describe	angiosperms as seed plants and the largest group, or division, in the Plant Kingdom	2
illustrate and compare	the size of the smallest and largest angiosperms: • smallest: duckweed • largest: giant eucalyptus tree	2
draw on a map	six examples of angiosperms found around the world	6
make a Venn diagram	comparing angiosperms and gymnosperms	3
compare	fruits and vegetables	2
explain	why some fruits are mistakenly called vegetables and give specific examples	2
investigate	two angiosperms that are parasites *example:* • Stinking Corpse Lily or Southeast Asia	2
sketch and label	the parts of an angiosperm, or flowering plant	any number

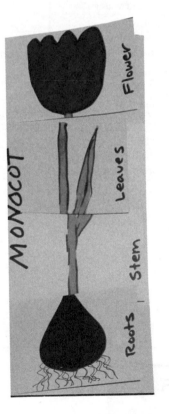

Three-tab book

Animals

Skill	Activity Suggestion	Foldable Parts
question	create a "know?-like to know? -learned" about animals	3
describe	animals and the Animal Kingdom	2
	animals as vertebrates or invertebrates	2
	animals as either warm-blooded (endothermic) or cold-blooded (ectothermic)	2
argue	advantages and disadvantages of being cold-blooded	2
	advantages and disadvantages of being warm-blooded	2
chart	animals by land (terrestrial) or water (aquatic) habitats	2
	animals common to each continent	7
	animals by at least four methods of locomotion • 2 legs • 4 legs • wings • fins	4
make a Venn diagram	comparing animals with backbones (vertebrates) and animals without backbones (invertebrates)	3
compare	animals with endoskeletons and exoskeletons	2
	young animals that do and do not have parental care	2
list	four characteristics of animals • composed of many cells • capable of voluntary movement • reproduce like organisms • adjust to surroundings	4
	examples of animals that are bipedal (2 legs) and animals that are quadrupedal (4 legs)	2
	examples of animals that are carnivores, herbivores, and omnivores	3
show	form and function of an animal's sense organ	2
diagram	animal life cycles	any number
summarize	animal respiration, including taking in oxygen and giving out carbon dioxide	2
explain	why some animals migrate and others do not	2
map and label	migratory routes of three different animal groups	3
	animal habitats where you live	any number
research and report on	at least three reasons animals become endangered: • loss of habitat • introduction of new species • pollution • human population growth • hunting, others	3+
	animals that are threatened, endangered, and extinct	3
chart	pros and cons of animals living in a community	2
define	frugivorous and insectivorous	2

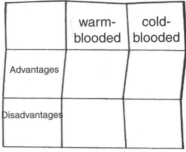

	warm-blooded	cold-blooded
Advantages		
Disadvantages		

3x3 Folded chart

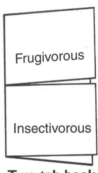

Frugivorous

Insectivorous

Two-tab book

Animal	Form	Function
Sight Organ		
Smell Organ		
Hearing Organ		

3x4 Folded chart

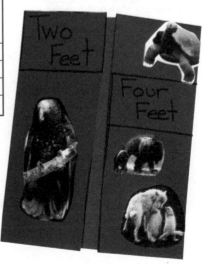

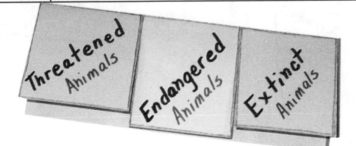

Arachnids

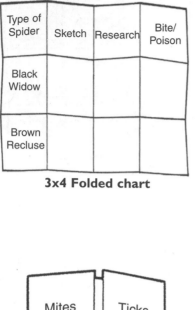

Type of Spider	Sketch	Research	Bite/ Poison
Black Widow			
Brown Recluse			

3x4 Folded chart

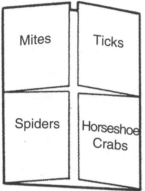

Mites	Ticks
Spiders	Horseshoe Crabs

Four-door book

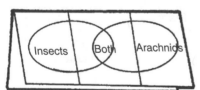

Insects Both Arachnids

Three-tab Venn diagram

Skill	Activity Suggestion	Foldable Parts
question	create a "know?-like to know? -learned" about arachnids	
describe	three characteristics of arachnids: • eight jointed legs • segmented bodies with two parts • thin exoskeletons	3
	four examples of arachnids: • mites • ticks • spiders • horseshoe crabs	4
make a Venn diagram	to compare insects and arachnids	3
diagram	spider body parts including cephalothorax and abdomen	2
create	an arachnid identification chart	any number
explain	why all spiders are poisonous but few are dangerous to humans	2
research	two spiders that are dangerous to humans: • black widow • brown recluse	2
	how hummingbirds use spider webs to build their nests	1
	one species of arachnid in terms of diet, size, habitat, length of life, and reproduction	5
	the "what" and "where" of Lyme disease	2
	the "who, what, where, when" of Dr. Thomas Muffet and his daughter "Little Miss Muffet"	4
prove	the statement "Daddy-long legs are not spiders."	1
observe	two spider webs, describe and sketch what you see	2
compare	orb and net spider webs	2
design an experiment	to determine the strength of a spider's web	any number
determine	and give examples of spiders that are harmful and spiders that are beneficial	2

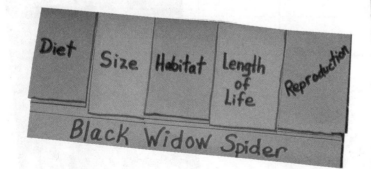

Diet | Size | Habitat | Length of Life | Reproduction

Black Widow Spider

ORB WEB   NET WEB

Asteroids

Skill	Activity Suggestion	Foldable Parts
question	create a "know?-like to know? -learned" about asteroids	3
describe	the asteroid belt and its position within the solar system	1
	asteroids inside and outside the asteroid belt	2
compare and contrast	the main types of asteroids: • stony • metal	2
diagram	the position of the asteroid belt in the solar system	1
explain	why asteroids are also called "minor planets" or "planetoids"	1
	how many asteroids have been discovered and how astronomers name asteroids	2
graph	three asteroid diameters: • Ceres, 623 miles • Pallas, 378 miles • Juno, 143 miles • Astraea, 73 miles • Phocaea, 45 miles, others	3
predict	what would happen if a large asteroid hit Earth	1
research	the discovery and naming of the first asteroid	2
	what is known about past asteroid collisions with Earth, possibly including Chicxulub on the Yucatan Peninsula	any number
	Kirkwood Gaps and Daniel Kirkwood	2
	the "who, what, when, where" of Giuseppe Piazzi	4
	the "who, what, when, where" of William Herschel	4

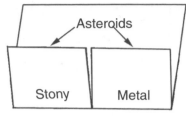

Two-tab concept map

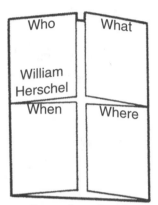

Four-door book

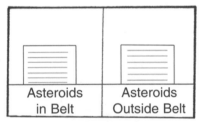

Pocket book

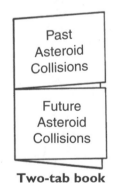

Two-tab book

Atmosphere

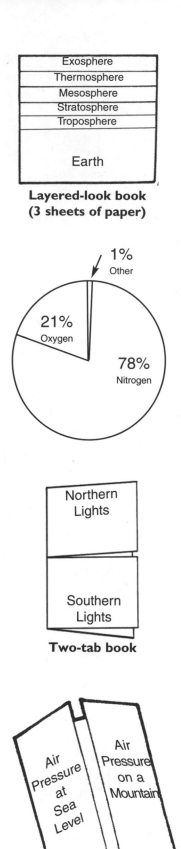

Exosphere
Thermosphere
Mesosphere
Stratosphere
Troposphere

Earth

**Layered-look book
(3 sheets of paper)**

1%
Other

21%
Oxygen

78%
Nitrogen

Northern
Lights

Southern
Lights

Two-tab book

Air
Pressure
at
Sea
Level

Air
Pressure
on a
Mountain

Shutter-fold book

Skill	Activity Suggestion	Foldable Parts
question	create a "know?-like to know? -learned" about the atmosphere	3
describe	Earth's atmosphere	1
	air pressure	1
sketch and label	the layers of Earth's atmosphere: • troposphere • stratosphere • mesosphere • thermosphere • exosphere	5
explain	why the troposphere is called the "weather" layer	1
	why density of the atmosphere decreases, or air gets thinner, as height increases	1
	two ways in which the atmosphere would differ if humans had never lived on Earth	2
	why the troposphere is the only layer in which life is found naturally	1
compare	the troposphere to another atmosphere layer	2
	air pressure at sea level and on a mountain top	2
graph	atmosphere composition: • nitrogen 78% • oxygen 21% • other gases 1%	3
list	the four most common atmospheric gases: • nitrogen • oxygen • argon • carbon dioxide	4
investigate	northern lights (aurora borealis) and southern lights (aurora australis)	2
research	five common and uncommon things (particulates) found in the atmosphere: • salt • smoke • dust • pollutants • pollen • volcanic ash, others	5
	the ozone layer in the stratosphere, its importance, and causes and effects of observed changes	3

Troposphere

Atoms and Molecules

Skill	Activity Suggestion	Foldable Parts
question	create a "know?-like to know? -learned" about atoms and molecules	3
define	an atom as the smallest part of an element that keeps the properties of the element	1
observe	a periodic table of elements, find elements you know or have heard of, and recall that every element has an atom that is different from every other element	any number
research	the "who, what, when, where" of John Dalton	4
	what is inside an atom: • protons • neutrons • electrons	3
	the "what" and "when" of quarks	2
describe	why atoms are mainly empty space	1
	the electric charges of protons and neutrons	2
	how the number of protons in an atom determines what element it is	1
make a concept map	illustrating the atomic nucleus composed of the protons and neutrons	2
draw or make	a model of a carbon atom and a hydrogen atom	2
make a time line	of the development of the atomic model	any number

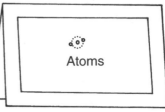

Picture-frame book

**Layered-look book
(2 sheets of paper)**

Bacteria

Skill	Activity Suggestion	Foldable Parts
question	create a "know?-like to know? -learned" about bacteria	
describe	bacteria	1
	all bacteria as prokaryotes	1
differentiate	between infection and disease	2
compare	beneficial bacteria and harmful bacteria	2
	bacteria that do and do not need air to exist (aerobes and anaerobes)	2
explain	why bacteria are often called "germs" and explain how to prevent the spread of bacteria or "germs"	2
cause and effect	of bacteria developing antibiotic resistance	2
make a time line	of the history of pasteurization	any number
diagram	the three basic shapes of bacteria: • coccus • spirillum • bacillus	3
research	what part bacteria play in cheese production	1
determine	diseases caused by bacteria	any number
	what role bacteria plays in biomes	any number

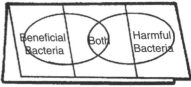

Four-door book

Three-tab Venn diagram

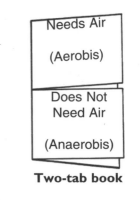

Two-tab book

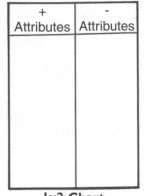

1x2 Chart

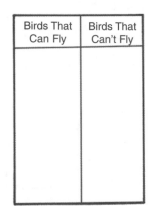

Three-tab Venn diagram

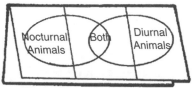

1x2 Chart

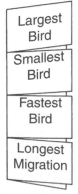

Four-tab book

Bats

Skill	Activity Suggestion	Foldable Parts
question	create a "know?-like to know? -learned" about bats	3
list	the positive and negative attributes of bats	2
describe	bats as nocturnal animals and compare them to a diurnal animal	2
	the form and function of bat wings	2
	the form and function of bat eyes	2
research	two species of bats common to the United States	2
map	the migratory route of one or more species of bats	any number
investigate	how bats maneuver in darkness and how bats locate their food	2
	the importance of bat guano--past and present	2
	the growth and development of bat young, or pup	2
compare	insectivorous and frugivorous bats	2

Birds

Skill	Activity Suggestion	Foldable Parts
question	create a "know?-like to know? -learned" about birds	3
compare and contrast	birds that can and cannot fly (ratites)	2
	nocturnal and diurnal birds	2
	the feet of an ostrich, penguin, and robin	3
	land birds and water birds	2
describe	physical characteristics of predatory birds and birds that are prey	2
	form and function of wings and feathers	2
list	four characteristics of birds • wings • beak • feathers • eggs	4
sketch	and describe the purpose of three different beaks	3
observe	bird behaviors and note bird calls and/or songs	2
research	birds that do and do not build nests	2
	record setting birds: largest, smallest, fastest, others	any number
show	how birds fit into two different food webs	2
investigate	the fossil record of birds	any number

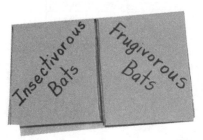

Butterflies and Moths

Skill	Activity Suggestion	Foldable Parts
question	create a "know?-like to know? -learned" about butterflies and moths	3
explain	three characteristics that identify butterflies and moths as insects	3
sketch	the life cycle of a butterfly: • egg • larva • pupa • adult	4
compare	the pupa stage of a butterfly and a moth	2
make a Venn diagram	to compare butterflies and moths	3
determine	if all butterflies are diurnal and all moths are nocturnal	2
describe	the form and function of butterfly and moth wings	2
draw and label	the body parts of moths and butterflies	2
map	the migratory route of a species of butterfly	1
chart	ways in which humans find butterflies and moths helpful and harmful	2

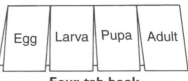

Four-tab book

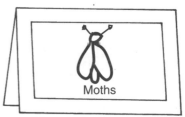

Picture-frame book

Caves

Skill	Activity Suggestion	Foldable Parts
question	create a "know?-like to know? -learned" about caves	3
describe	three or more steps in the formation of a cave	3+
sketch	the cross section of a cave and label formations	any number
compare	dry and wet cave systems	2
	past and present uses of cave systems by humankind	2
debate	pros and cons of cave systems being opened to tourism	2
diagram	stalactites, stalagmites, and cave columns	3
determine	carbonic acid's effect on limestone	1
research	solution caves, sea caves, and lava caves	3
map	locations of cave systems around the world	any number
make a model	of a cave system showing light zone, twilight zone and midnight zone	3
report on	two troglobites: blind or eyeless cave animals	2
	four unique speleothems such as drapery, flowstone, gypsum flowers, fried eggs, or helictites	4
	endangered cave life	any number
show cause and effect	of groundwater erosion and cave formation	2

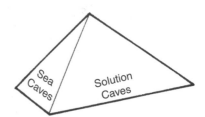

Pyramid fold

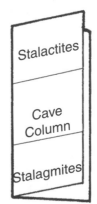

Three-tab book

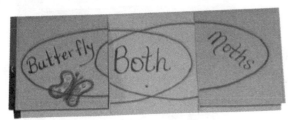

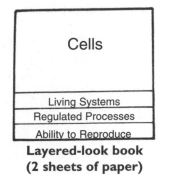

Cells

Living Systems
Regulated Processes
Ability to Reproduce

**Layered-look book
(2 sheets of paper)**

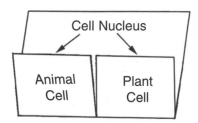

Cell Nucleus

Animal
Cell

Plant
Cell

Two-tab concept map

Cloud
Observation
Journal

Bound book

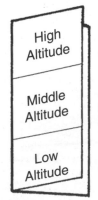

High
Altitude

Middle
Altitude

Low
Altitude

Three-tab book

Cells

Skill	Activity Suggestion	Foldable Parts
question	create a "know?-like to know? -learned" about cells	3
define	cell as a basic unit of life and compare cells to building blocks	2
explain	the cell theory	1
describe	cells: • living systems • regulated processes • ability to reproduce	any number
diagram	form and function of the nucleus of a cell	2
compare and contrast	eukaryotic and prokaryotic cells	2
	plant and animal cells	2
	tissue and organs	2
	mitosis and meiosis	2
research	largest and smallest cells	2
	the "who, what, when, where" of Robert Hooke	4

Clouds

Skill	Activity Suggestion	Foldable Parts
question	create a "know?-like to know? -learned" about clouds	3
chart	your own cloud cover classification system *examples:* clear, scattered, broken, overcast, others	any number
make	a cloud identification chart	1
observe	cloud shapes and movement	2
record	types of clouds observed over a period of time	any number
compare	clouds that do and do not produce rain	2
summarize	how smog forms	1
describe	cloud formation at these different levels: • low-altitude • middle-altitude • high-altitude	3
explain	cloud colors	1
	the classification of clouds into three large categories: • cirrus • cumulus • stratus	3
research	the "who, what, when, where" of Luke Howard	4

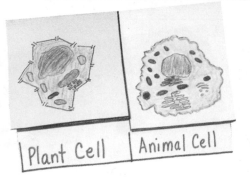

Plant Cell   Animal Cell

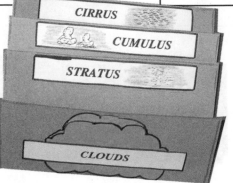

CIRRUS

CUMULUS

STRATUS

CLOUDS

Color

Skill	Activity Suggestion	Foldable Parts
question	create a "know?-like to know? -learned" about color	3
compare and contrast	primary pigment colors and primary light colors	2
find and list	example of materials that are the primary colors: red, yellow, and blue	3
explain	how secondary colors are formed: • red and yellow form the secondary color orange • red and blue form the secondary color purple • blue and yellow form the secondary color green	3
diagram	a spectrum, including red, orange, yellow, green, blue, indigo, and violet	7
	a color wheel showing primary and secondary colors	6
describe	the relationship between color and light	1

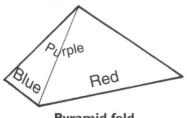

Pyramid fold

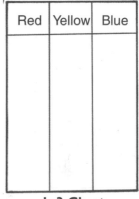

1x3 Chart

Comets

Skill	Activity Suggestion	Foldable Parts
question	create a "know?-like to know? -learned" about comets	3
diagram	the parts of a comet: • nucleus • coma • tail(s)	3
compare	a short-period and long-period comet	2
explain	why a comet's tail always points away from the Sun and describe solar winds	2
make a model	of a comet	1
make a time line	of comets viewed throughout history	any number
research	the composition of a comet	any number
	modern and historic comets	2
	the "who, what, when, where" of : • Edmond Halley • Jean Louis Pons • Fred Lawrence Whipple • Carolyn Shoemaker, others	4
make a table	of information on three known comets	3

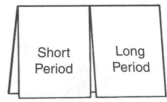

Two-tab book

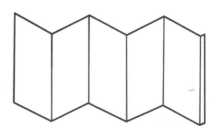

**Time line:
Comets Viewed Through
History**

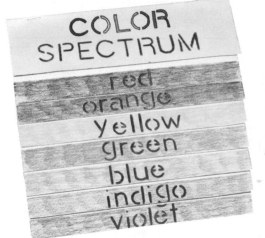

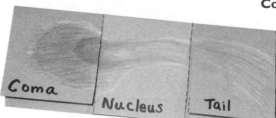

Desert

Deserts
Antarctica
Asia
Africa
Europe
North America
South America
Australia

**Layered-look book
(4 sheets of paper)**

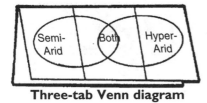

Four-tab book

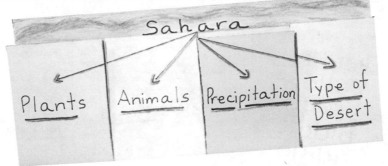

Three-tab Venn diagram

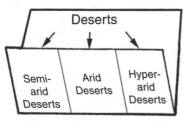

Three-tab concept map

Skill	Activity Suggestion	Foldable Parts
question	create a "know?-like to know? -learned" about deserts	3
locate	the major deserts of each continent on a map	7
describe	three conditions that determine a desert	3
	desert weathering including water and wind	2
	three ways in which desert plants reduce water loss: • reduced size of leaf or spine • waxy coating on leaves or stems • leaves that fold or close	3
	how the following desert animals have adapted to little water and high daytime temperatures: • camels • kangaroo rat • rattlesnakes	3
explain	deserts as "lands of extremes"	1
	the existence of polar deserts	1
graph	the percentage of the world's land that is and is not desert	2
	examples of night and day temperature variations in a desert	2
make a table	on desert insects, arachnids, fish, amphibians, reptiles, birds, and mammals	any number
	of information on weather conditions in several deserts, including precipitation, windstorms, evaporation rate, humidity levels, and others	any number
research	three or four different types of deserts: • sand dunes • rock • pebbled ground • frozen	4
report on	four common desert plants: • cacti • yucca • mesquite • sagebrush • creosote bush, others	4
	four common desert animals: • reptiles • arachnids • small mammals • birds, others	4
differentiate	between semiarid deserts, arid deserts, and hyperarid deserts	3
investigate	past and present peoples of the desert	2

Dinosaurs

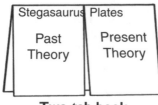

Skill	Activity Suggestion	Foldable Parts
question	create a "know?-like to know? -learned" about dinosaurs	3
chart	meat-eaters and plant-eaters	2
compare and contrast	the movement of animals with an upright posture to those with a sprawling posture	2
	several of the giant plant-eating dinosaurs	any number
	Megalosaurus, Giganotosaurus, Carcharodontosaurus, and Tyrannosaurus rex and graph by size	4
	dinosaur movement, including bipedal, quadrupedal, and facultative (movement using both two and four feet)	3
	the sizes of dinosaur eggs to living animals	2
	past and present theories on the purpose of Stegosaurus's plates	2
debate	the statement "There are some things we will never know conclusively about dinosaurs, such as skin color, sounds, smells, and mannerisms."	1
discuss	the cause and consequence of being a gigantotherm	2
	a dinosaur extinction theory	1
explain	geologic time as it relates to dinosaurs	any number
	the importance of fossilized feces	1
	why most dinosaur fossils are usually found in areas of deposition, such as rivers, lakes, or deltas	1
graph	dinosaur sizes from smallest to largest known	any number
	length of dinosaur body parts, possibly including necks, tails, claws, heads, plates, others	any number
illustrate	and describe the following animals that are often incorrectly called dinosaurs *example:* Dimetrodon, pterosaurs, and swimming reptiles	3
	outlines of different-shaped dinosaur teeth	any number
list	advantages and disadvantages of dinosaurs being cold blooded and warm blooded	2
	advantages and disadvantages of different dinosaur defense techniques, including armor, scutes, horns, whiplike tails, giant size, others	2
make a time line	of the Mesozoic Era	any number
make a Venn diagram	labeled carnivorous, herbivorous, omnivorous	3
	labeled predators, scavengers, and possibly both	3
	labeled bipedal, quadrupedal, and facultative (both)	3
outline	the commercialization of dinosaurs since they were first named in 1842	any number
research	the two divisions that contain nearly all known dinosaurs--Saurischia and Ornithischia	2
	the past and present views of dinosaur stances, including tail position and posture	2
	the importance of ichnites (petrified footprints) and track ways	2
	flora and fauna of the Triassic, Jurassic, and Cretaceous periods of the Mesozoic Era	3
	mummified dinosaurs	any number
	famous fossilized nesting sites, called rookeries	any number
report on	the "who, what, when, where" of a paleontologist: Richard Owen, Charles Marsh, Edward Cope, others	4

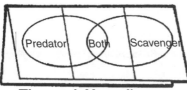

Two-tab book

Three-tab Venn diagram

3x4 Folded chart

Layered-look book (3 sheets of paper)

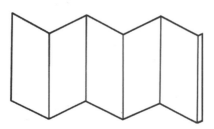

Time line: of the Mesozoic Era

Earth

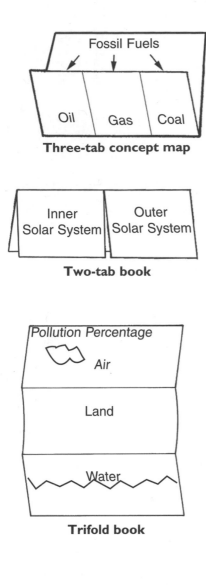

Three-tab concept map

Fossil Fuels

Oil | Gas | Coal

Two-tab book

Inner Solar System | Outer Solar System

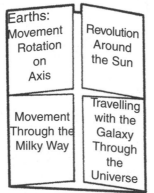

Trifold book

Pollution Percentage
Air
Land
Water

Four-door book

Earths: Movement Rotation on Axis | Revolution Around the Sun

Movement Through the Milky Way | Travelling with the Galaxy Through the Universe

Skill	Activity Suggestion	Foldable Parts
question	create a "know?-like to know? -learned" about Earth	3
describe	Earth as your home	1
	Earth's shape as it relates to polar and equatorial circumference	2
diagram	Earth as an inner planet in the solar system	1
	a cross section of Earth's including inner core, outer core, mantle, and crust	4
graph	Earth's surface area: • 70.8% water, or about 3/4ths • 29.2% land, or about 1/4th	2
make a time line	of Earth's geological development and change	any number
investigate	ancient myths and folklore about Earth's formation	any number
	Earth's three main fossil fuels: • oil • gas • coal	3
research	Earth's movement: • rotation on its axis • revolution around the Sun • movement through the Milky Way Galaxy • traveling with the galaxy through the universe	4
	how Earth's size is measured	1
	how Earth's age is determined	1
	the percentage of pollution in the air, land and water	3

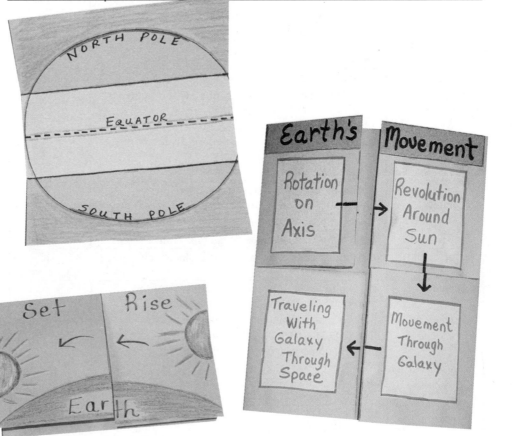

Earthquakes

Skill	Activity Suggestion	Foldable Parts
question	create a "know?-like to know? -learned" about earthquakes	3
describe	an imaginary town before and after an earthquake	2
	how earthquakes are measured: • Richter Scale • Mercalli Scale	2
	recent and historic earthquakes	2
diagram	an earthquake	1
investigate	the earthquake belt that circles the Pacific Ocean and the earthquake belt that stretches from the Mediterranean and north Africa into Southern Asia	2
	building materials made for earthquake regions	any number
report on	recent and historic tsunamis	2
show cause and effect	of plate tectonics and earthquakes	2
	of the San Andreas fault	2
write	an earthquake safety manual	1
research	past and present methods for predicting earthquakes	2
make a Venn diagram	labeled earthquakes, tsunamis, and both	3

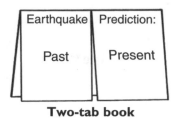

Two-tab book

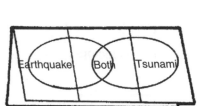

Three-tab Venn diagram

Eggs

Skill	Activity Suggestion	Foldable Parts
question	create a "know?-like to know? -learned" about eggs	3
observe	and diagram the parts of a chicken egg: • yolk • albumen (white) • membranes • shell	4
research	vertebrates that lay eggs--birds, reptiles, amphibians, and fish	4
	two mammals that lay eggs--echidna and platypus	2
	two invertebrates that lay eggs	2
compare	bird eggs: largest (ostrich) and smallest (hummingbird)	2
determine	advantages and disadvantages of eggs laid on land and eggs laid in water	2
describe	three characteristics of amniotic eggs: • hard-shelled • embryo surrounded by a liquid • amniotic sac/membrane	3

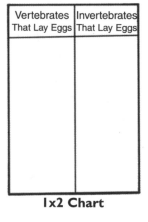

1x2 Chart

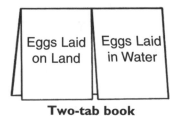

Two-tab book

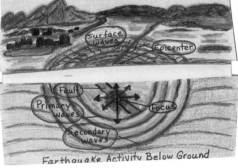

Electricity

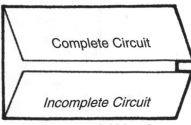

Complete Circuit

Incomplete Circuit

Shutter-fold book

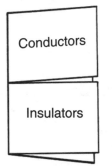

Conductors

Insulators

Two-tab book

Skill	Activity Suggestion	Foldable Parts
question	create a "know?-like to know? -learned" about electricity	3
list	four ways you use electricity everyday	4
imagine	and write about what your town was like before electricity	1
define	electricity, static electricity, volt, ampere, ohm, watt, watt-hour, kilowatt-hour	any number
diagram	a simple electric circuit: • source • path • result	3
	parts of a light bulb	any number
explain	an electric current as the flow of negative electrons	2
	the uses of conductors and insulators	2
compare	a complete and incomplete circuit	2
describe	how electric current is generated by an energy source such as oil, gas, coal, or nuclear power	any number
research	the "who, what, when, where" of Benjamin Franklin, Alessandro Volta, John Ambrose Fleming, others	4
	the generation of electricity using water, wind, and solar sources	3

Electromagnetism

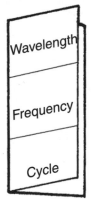

Wavelength

Frequency

Cycle

Three-tab book

Skill	Activity Suggestion	Foldable Parts
question	create a "know?-like to know? -learned" about electromagnets and electromagnetism	3
define	wavelength, frequency, and cycle	3
compare and contrast	waves that need matter to transfer energy and those that do not need matter to transfer energy	2
	invisible and visible electromagnetic waves	2
	electromagnetic and particle radiation	2
describe	what happens to ultraviolet rays entering Earth's atmosphere: are or are not absorbed by ozone layer	2
diagram	the electromagnetic wave spectrum	7
explain	what happens when electromagnetic waves hit a solid, liquid, or a gas	3
research	any of the following: AM waves, FM waves, microwave, X rays, gamma rays, infrared waves	any number
	the "who, what, when, where" of Joseph Henry, Robert Bunsen, James Maxwell, Heinrich Hertz	4

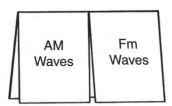

AM Waves

Fm Waves

Two-tab book

SOURCE   PATH   RESULT

Elements

Skill	Activity Suggestion	Foldable Parts
question	create a "know?-like to know? -learned" about elements	3
determine	how many elements have been discovered or created and officially named	1
differentiate	between elements, compounds, and mixtures	3
graph	the most common elements: • in Earth's crust • in Earth's air • in ocean water	3
explain	why hydrogen is the most common element in the universe	1
investigate	how elements are organized using the Periodic Table	1

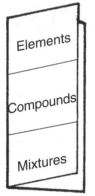

Three-tab book

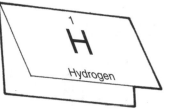

Half book

Energy

Skill	Activity Suggestion	Foldable Parts
question	create a "know?-like to know? -learned" about energy	3
compare and contrast	kinds of energy: • kinetic energy • potential energy	2
	renewable and nonrenewable energy sources	2
	energy efficient and inefficient tools and machines	2
discuss	"Every change in the universe represents the change of energy from one form to another."	1
	why energy cannot be created or destroyed, but can be transferred from one piece of matter to another	1
show effects	of two different energy transformations	2
explain	how kinetic energy can become potential and potential energy can become kinetic	2
list	three or more forms of energy	3+
research	the "who, what, when, where" of: Gustave Coriolis, James Prescott Joule, Hermann Ludwig von Helmholtz, Albert Einstein, others	4

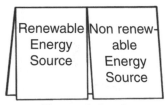

Two-tab book

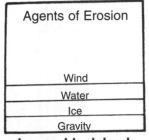

Agents of Erosion

Wind
Water
Ice
Gravity

**Layered-look book
(2 sheets of paper)**

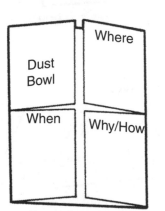

Where

Dust
Bowl

When

Why/How

Four-door book

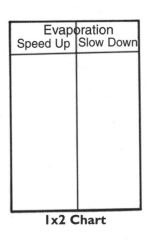

Evaporation
Speed Up | Slow Down

1x2 Chart

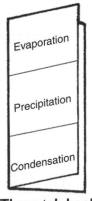

Evaporation

Precipitation

Condensation

Three-tab book

Erosion and Deposition

Skill	Activity Suggestion	Foldable Parts
question	create a "know?-like to know? -learned" about erosion	3
describe	the beneficial and harmful effects of erosion and deposition	2
	the agents of erosion: • wind • water • ice • gravity	4
	the cause and effect of wave erosion	2
discuss	three ways erosion shapes Earth's surface	3
observe	and describe two locations where erosion is occurring in your community	2
explain	how humans can speed up or slow down the natural process of erosion	2
investigate	four types of mass movements: creep, slump, rock slides, and mudflows	4
	the following: beach erosion, cave formation, glacial erosion, and agricultural erosion	4
research	the "what, when, where, why" of the 1930's Dust Bowl and/or the formation of the Mississippi delta	4

Evaporation

Skill	Activity Suggestion	Foldable Parts
question	create a "know?-like to know? -learned" about evaporation	3
describe	evaporation as the change of a liquid to a gas	1
observe	that a wet paper towel exposed to air will dry and document the process	any number
explain	the water cycle and describe the part evaporation plays: • evaporation of water • condensation • precipitation	3
investigate	plant transpiration as it relates to evaporation and condensation	2
determine	ways in which evaporation can be decreased up or increased	2
imagine	what Earth would be like without evaporation	1

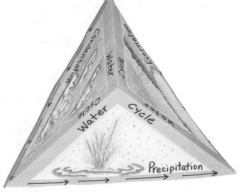

Ferns

Skill	Activity Suggestion	Foldable Parts
question	create a "know?-like to know? -learned" about ferns	3
observe	a fern leaf or frond and describe what you see	any number
diagram	the following parts of a fern: • stem • roots • leaves	3
	the life cycle of a fern: sexual and asexual stages	2
list	three characteristics of ferns: • green plants • nonflowering • found in most biomes	3
	pros and cons of spore reproduction	2
differentiate	between fertile and sterile fern leaves	2
explain	the importance of ferns to the formation of coal and the economic impact prehistoric plants like ferns still have on the world economy	2
research	tree-sized ferns found in Hawaii and explain why ferns can grow taller than mosses	2

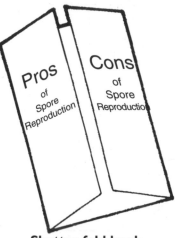

Shutter-fold book

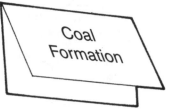

Half book

Fish

Skill	Activity Suggestion	Foldable Parts
question	create a "know?-like to know? -learned" about fish	3
compare	bony and cartilaginous fish	2
	cold blooded fish to warm blooded animals	2
create	a shark identification chart	1
diagram	a fish food chain and a food web	2
	a fish and its fins: • anal • dorsal • caudal	3
explain	how a fish breathes under water	1
	why the Devonian period of the Paleozoic Era is called the "Age of Fishes"	1
	why jellyfish and shellfish are not really fish	2
graph	fish sizes: smallest to largest	any number
list	examples of freshwater and saltwater fish	2
observe	fish scales and describe their form and function	2
	fish swimming in an aquarium and record observations	1
research	the classes of fish: jawless, cartilaginous, and bony	3
	the "what, when, where" of the coelacanth	3
	lung fish and estivation	2

Bound book

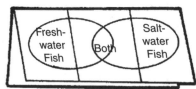

Three-tab Venn diagram

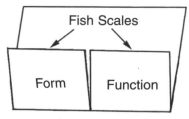

Two-tab concept map

Flowers

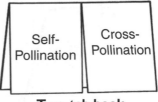

Two-tab book

Skill	Activity Suggestion	Foldable Parts
question	create a "know?-like to know? -learned" about flowers	3
observe	and record flower colors, sizes, shapes, and locations	4
determine	three characteristics all flowers have in common	3
diagram	the parts of a flower: anther, stigma, filament, style, pistil, petals, sepals, and ovary	8
	and compare self-pollination and cross-pollination	2
	and explain the three main steps of fertilization: • pollen lands on stigma and a pollen tube grows • pollen tube grows into ovary to reach an egg cell • sperm moves down the tube to fertilize the egg	3
explain	how flowers differ: • complete flowers: sepals, petals, stamens, pistils • incomplete flowers: are missing one of these parts • perfect flowers: have both pistils and stamens or male and female parts	3

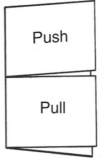

**Layered-look book
(2 sheets of paper)**

Forces

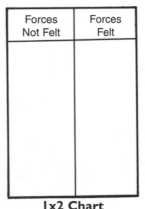

Two-tab book

Skill	Activity Suggestion	Foldable Parts
question	create a "know?-like to know? -learned" about forces	3
define	a force as a push or pull that one object exerts on another	1
compare and contrast	balanced and unbalanced forces	2
describe	how force, mass, and acceleration are related	3
design	an activity that demonstrates centripetal force	1
explain	how forces can change motion	1
	how Newton's 2nd and 3rd laws of motion relate to forces	2
research	forces that are and are not felt	2

1x2 Chart

Fossils

Skill	Activity Suggestion	Foldable Part
question	create a "know?-like to know? -learned" about fossils	3
describe	types of fossils by their formation, including mold, cast, petrified, and carbon film	4
compare	trace fossils and body fossils	2
	mineralized fossils and cast fossils	2
explain	how ancient life forms can be preserved in ice, permafrost, bogs, and tar	4
	in what type of rock most fossils are found	1
illustrate	the formation of mold and cast fossils	2
outline	steps for fossilization including death, decay, burial, and mineralization	4
research	four vertebrate trace fossils: eggs, tracks, coprolites, skin imprints, gastroliths, others	4
	"what" and "how" of the principle of superposition	2
	two ways in which fossils are dated	2

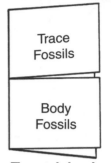

Two-tab book

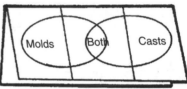

Three-tab Venn diagram

Friction

Skill	Activity Suggestion	Foldable Part
question	create a "know?-like to know? -learned" about friction	3
compare	a world with and without friction	2
	friction produced by rough and smooth surfaces	2
demonstrate	how friction works to make things stop moving while producing heat	1
describe	three types of friction: • static • sliding • rolling	3
	three lubricants that reduce friction	3
list	ways to increase and decrease friction	2
	the beneficial and harmful effects of friction	2
write	about "frictional" encounters during an average day	any number

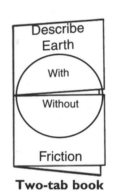

Two-tab book

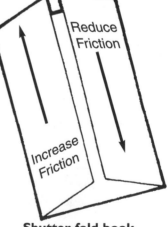

Shutter-fold book

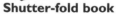

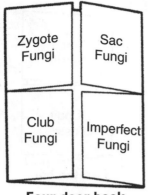

Four-door book

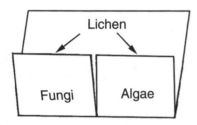

Two-tab concept map

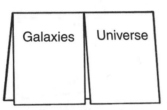

Two-tab book

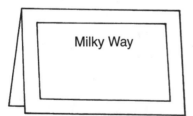

Picture-frame book

Fungi

Skill	Activity Suggestion	Foldable Parts
question	create a "know?-like to know? -learned" about fungus	3
classify	fungi by the structure in which they produce spores: • zygote fungi • sac fungi • club fungi • imperfect fungi	4
find	three examples of fungi around you: • yeast used to make bread dough rise • mold on bread or fruit • mushrooms	3
develop	a mushroom identification chart	any number
diagram	parts of fungi	any number
research	the symbiotic relationship between fungi and algae that form lichen	2
	positive and negative effects of fungi	2

Galaxies

Skill	Activity Suggestion	Foldable Parts
question	create a "know?-like to know? -learned" about galaxies	3
explain	how galaxies form the universe	1
compare and contrast	barred spiral galaxies and unbarred spirals	2
	galactic clusters and globular clusters	2
describe	irregular, spiral, and elliptical galaxies	3
	the Milky Way and its place in the universe	2
research	four discoveries of the Hubble Space Telescope	4
	the use of light-years as a unit of measurement in space	1
	the "who, what, when, where" of Harlow Shapley	4
	the "what" and "where" of the Local Group	2

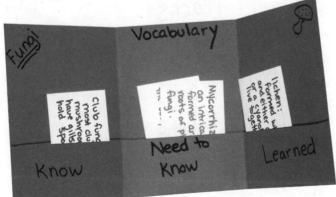

Gases

Skill	Activity Suggestion	Foldable Parts
question	create a "know?-like to know? -learned" about gases	3
describe	gases as one of the four states of matter	1
	two characteristics of gases: • no definite size • no definite shape	2
compare	gases to liquids and gases to solids	2
find	examples of three gases on the Periodic Table	3
explain	the importance of the following gases to life on Earth: • oxygen • nitrogen	2
	why helium gas is used to inflate balloons	1
	what happens to gases when they are heated and cooled	2
discover	three things dependent upon gases for inflation	3
describe	gases and liquids as fluids	2

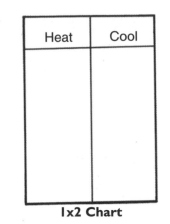

1x2 Chart

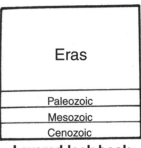

Shutter-fold book

Geologic Time

Skill	Activity Suggestion	Foldable Parts
question	create a "know?-like to know? -learned" about geologic time	3
define	eon, era, period, and epoch	4
make	a geologic time scale	any number
chart	and describe each of the following three eras: • Paleozoic • Mesozoic • Cenozoic	3
diagram	the movement of Earth's plates during the Paleozoic, Mesozoic, and Cenozoic eras	3
compare	relative time scales and numerical time scales	2
research	the "who, what, when, where" of Bertman B. Boltwood and Alfred Wegener	4

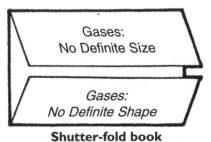

**Layered-look book
(2 sheets of paper)**

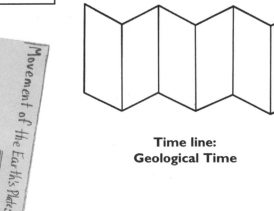

**Time line:
Geological Time**

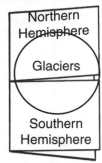

Two-tab book

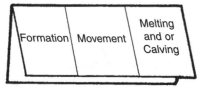

Three-tab book

Glaciers

Skill	Activity Suggestion	Foldable Parts
question	create a "know?-like to know? -learned" about glaciers	3
outline	the formation of a glacier	any number
compare and contrast	valley glaciers, ice sheets, and ice shelves	3
	past and present glacial coverage of Earth's surface	2
	icebergs in the northern and southern oceans	2
demonstrate	ice floats because it is less dense than water	1
investigate	how glaciers collect and deposit debris	2
describe	Long Island as a glacial moraine	1
diagram and explain	the life of a glacier, including formation, movement, melting, and/or calving	3
show cause and effect	of glacial movement	2
predict	what would happen if glacial melting accelerated	1
research	glacial moraines, glacial lakes, and erratics	3

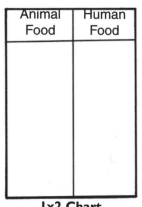

1x2 Chart

Grass

Skill	Activity Suggestion	Foldable Parts
question	create a "know?-like to know? -learned" about grass	3
report on	three different kinds of grasses	3
describe	four ways in which grass is important to life on Earth	4
	two ways in which grass can reproduce or spread: • seeds • rhizomes	2
determine	what part grasses play in feeding the world: • act as food for animals • act as food for humans	2

Half book

Gravity

Skill	Activity Suggestion	Foldable Parts
question	create a "know?-like to know? -learned" about gravity	3
list	three things that gravity affects on Earth *examples:* • keeping objects earthbound • water seeking the lowest point • objects falling to Earth • moving groundwater • causing erosion, others	3
imagine	what would happen to the Universe without gravity	1
discover	the center of gravity of four objects	4
	the effect of mass and distance on gravitational pull	2
	how Earth's gravity affects the Moon	1
explain	the law of universal gravitation: the force of gravity between two objects is affected by the amount of matter in the objects and the distance between the objects	1

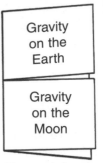

Two-tab book

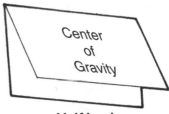

Half book

Gymnosperms

Skill	Activity Suggestion	Foldable Parts
question	create a "know?-like to know? -learned" about gymnosperms	3
compare	gymnosperms (do not produce flowers) and angiosperms (produce flowers)	2
describe	the four divisions of gymnosperms: • conifers • cycads • gnetophytes • ginkgoes	4
explain	two ways in which gymnosperms are adapted to cold, dry climates	2
investigate	the "what" and "where" of bristlecone pines	2
list	important products from gymnosperms, including resins, seeds, lumber, and mulch	4
diagram	gymnosperm leaves and cones	2

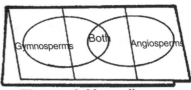

Three-tab Venn diagram

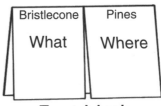

Two-tab book

Four-tab book

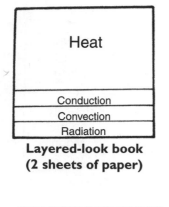

Heat

**Layered-look book
(2 sheets of paper)**

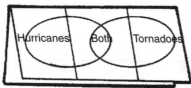

Reflect Heat Energy | Absorb Heat Energy

Two-tab book

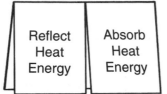

Hurricanes | Both | Tornadoes

Three-tab Venn diagram

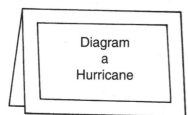

Diagram a Hurricane

Picture-frame book

Heat

Skill	Activity Suggestion	Foldable Parts
question	create a "know?-like to know? -learned" about heat	3
illustrate	heat transfer, which is energy moving from places with high temperature to places with lower temperatures	1
compare and contrast	light energy and heat energy from the Sun	2
	conduction, convection, and radiation	3
	materials used as conductors and insulators	2
	the use of Fahrenheit and Celsius	2
describe	surfaces that reflect and absorb heat energy	2
	air as a good insulator and poor conductor	2
design	an energy-efficient house that will have little heat loss	1
explain	boiling and freezing temperatures	2

Hurricane

Skill	Activity Suggestion	Foldable Parts
question	create a "know?-like to know? -learned" about hurricanes	3
compare	hurricanes and tornadoes	2
	hurricanes and typhoons	2
investigate	four recent hurricanes	4
track	a hurricane's movement using longitude and latitude	1
diagram	the cross-section of a hurricane and label	2
explain	two conditions needed for a hurricane to form	2
	how hurricanes are tracked, named, and classified	3

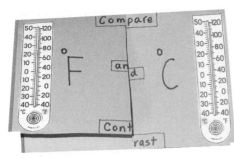

Hurricane Name	Location	Classification	Date
Andrew	South Florida Gulf of Mexico SE Louisiana	5	1992
Opal	Gulf Coast Florida panhandle	3	1995
Floyd			

Ice

Skill	Activity Suggestion	Foldable Parts
question	create a "know?-like to know? -learned" about ice	3
explain	why ice floats	1
illustrate	an iceberg and label what percent is above (10%) and below (90%) the water's surface	2
investigate	what percent of Earth's surface is covered by ice: • 10% of the land • 12% of the ocean	2
compare	ice at the North Pole and the South Pole	2
describe	how snow falling in central Antarctica will eventually be at the edge of the continent and possibly part of an iceberg at sea	1
make a time line	of the Ice Ages	any number

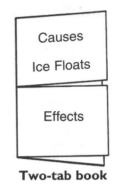

Two-tab book

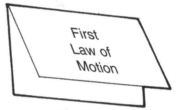

Time line:
of the Ice Ages

Inertia

Skill	Activity Suggestion	Foldable Parts
question	create a "know?-like to know? -learned" about inertia	3
define	inertia in the following ways: • objects at rest tend to stay at rest • objects moving tend to continue moving	2
	inertia as a property of matter and mass as a measure of inertia	2
describe	how the combined effects of gravity and inertia keep the Moon in orbit around Earth, and Earth in orbit around the Sun	2
outline	Sir Isaac Newton's first law of motion	1
research	the reasons for adding headrests and seat belts to cars	2

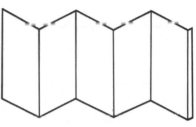

Half book

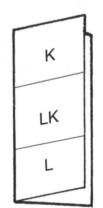

Three-tab book

Insects

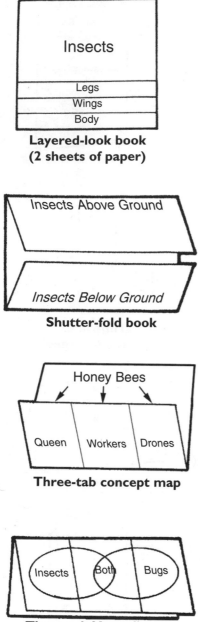

Layered-look book
(2 sheets of paper)

Insects Above Ground

Insects Below Ground

Shutter-fold book

Honey Bees

Queen | Workers | Drones

Three-tab concept map

Insects | Both | Bugs

Three-tab Venn diagram

Skill	Activity Suggestion	Foldable Parts
question	create a "know?-like to know? -learned" about insects	3
list	characteristics of insects including: • three pairs of jointed legs • three body parts • exoskeleton • one or two pairs of wings	any number
collect	dead insects, observe, identify, and label	any number
compare and contrast	chewing insects and sucking insects	2
	insects with two and four wings	2
	complete and incomplete metamorphosis	2
create	an insect identification chart	any number
debate	the pros and cons of using pesticides to kill insects	2
describe	insect legs	1
	how insects can be transferred from one habitat to another	1
diagram	insect body parts: • head • thorax • abdomen	3
give	three reasons insects are such successful animals	3
infer	why insects have remained relatively small in size	1
list	positive and negative outcomes of collecting insects for money and sport	2
	examples of nocturnal and diurnal insects	2
make a table	of different insects, possibly including size, diet, habitat, and life span	any number
make a Venn diagram	labeled insects, arachnids, and both	3
	labeled insects, bugs, and both	3
research	exoskeleton, chitin, molting	3
	honeybees, including workers, drones, and queens	3
	and compare social insects such as ants and honeybees	2
	brine flies and explain why they are so unusual	2
explain	how insects are beneficial and harmful to agriculture	2

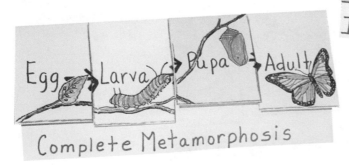

Egg → Nymph → Adult

Incomplete Metamorphosis

Egg → Larva → Pupa → Adult

Complete Metamorphosis

Invertebrates

Skill	Activity Suggestion	Foldable Parts
question	create a "know?-like to know? -learned" about invertebrates	3
compare and contrast	vertebrates and invertebrates	2
	invertebrates living on land and in water	2
graph	the ratio of invertebrates to vertebrates (about 90 percent to 10 percent)	2
investigate	any of the following groups of invertebrates: • jellyfish, coral, sea fans, and sea anemones • sponges • planarians, flatworms • roundworms • ribbon worm • earthworms • arrow worms • insects • shrimp, crabs, lobster, crayfish, barnacles, others • centipedes, millipedes • spiders • sand dollars, sea urchins, sea stars, sea cucumbers • clams, mussels, octopuses, oysters, snails, squids	any number

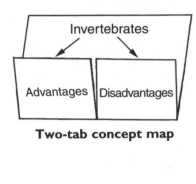

Two-tab concept map

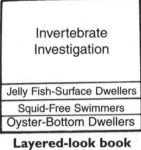

**Layered-look book
(2 sheets of paper)**

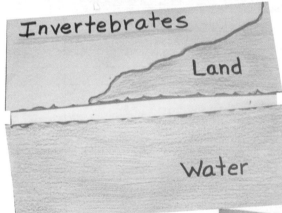

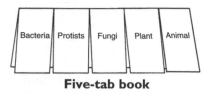

Five-tab book

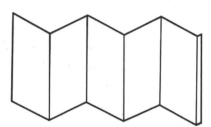

**Accordion fold:
Classification of Living
Organisms**

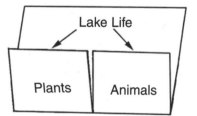

Two-tab book

Kingdoms

Skill	Activity Suggestion	Foldable Parts
question	create a "know?-like to know? -learned" about the six Kingdoms of living organisms	3
chart	examples of organisms from each Kingdom: • Archaebacteria • Eubacteria • Protista • Fungi • Plant • Animal	6
explain	why the number of Kingdoms can change	1
define	biology as the study of living organisms	1
outline	two or more characteristics organisms in all Kingdoms have in common	2+
make a time line	on the classification of living organisms	any number

Lake

Skill	Activity Suggestion	Foldable Parts
question	create a "know?-like to know? -learned" about lakes	3
compare	freshwater lakes and salt water lakes	2
	human-made and natural lakes	2
	ponds and lakes	2
outline	three features of natural lakes: • little water flow • most are freshwater • constantly filling with sediment	3
illustrate	seasonal changes in a lake	4
describe	three ways in which lakes influence people's lives	3
explain	two ways lakes can influence weather (lake-effect)	2
investigate	lake plants, vertebrate animals, invertebrate animals	3
report on	a salt lake: Great Salt Lake, Dead Sea, Caspian Sea	any number
	a freshwater lake: Siberia's Lake Baikal, Great Lakes of North America, the Great Lakes of Africa's Rift Valley, Mexico's ancient Lake Texcoco, others	any number

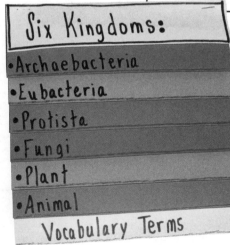

Land Forms

Skill	Activity Suggestion	Foldable Parts
question	create a "know?-like to know? -learned" about Earth's land forms	3
describe	the three main land forms: • plains • plateaus • mountains	3
make a diorama	of plants and animals found in a specific mountain, plains, or plateau ecosystem	any number
diagram	levels of plant and animal life on a mountain	any number
	major mountains, plains, and plateaus of a world map	3
explain	the life cycle of a mountain: young, mature, old	3
	the life cycle of a plateau: young, mature, old	3
research	two volcanic mountains	2
	different kinds of plains: coastal, interior, and lake	3
	Mid-Atlantic ridge (world's longest mountain chain)	1

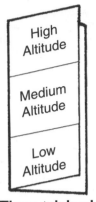

Three-tab book

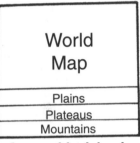

**Layered-look book
(2 sheets of paper)**

Leaves

Skill	Activity Suggestion	Foldable Parts
question	create a "know?-like to know? -learned" about leaves	3
collect	ten leaves of different shapes and sizes	10
describe and	simple and compound leaves	2
compare	leaves and thorns	2
diagram	the cross-section of a leaf	any number
compare	rain forest leaves with drip points and the leaves of a conifer	2
list	and describe five leaves you eat	5
explain	how leaves produce food by a process called photosynthesis	1
	the purpose of the cuticle on a leaf's surface	1
	cause and effect of leaves turning colors and dropping	2
research	the following leaves: tea, tobacco, and poinsettia	3
	the "who, what, when, where" of Stephen Hales	4

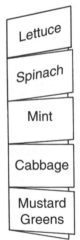

Five-tab book

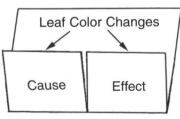

Two-tab concept map

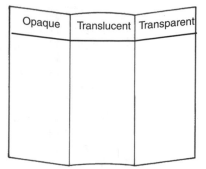

Trifold book

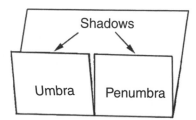

Two-tab concept map

Vocabulary book

Bound book

Light

Skill	Activity Suggestion	Foldable Parts
question	create a "know?-like to know? -learned" about light	3
describe	opaque, translucent, and transparent	3
compare and contrast	objects that are luminous and objects that are illuminated	2
	reflected light and refracted light	2
make a Venn diagram	to compare the human eye to a camera and determine what they have in common (both)	2
list	things that are and are not naturally luminous	2
observe	light reflecting off rough and smooth surfaces	2
diagram	shadows, including umbra and penumbra	2
	a spectrum including red, orange, yellow, green, blue, indigo, and violet	7
	an incident ray, angle of incidence, and angle of reflection	3
research	the measurement of long distances using the light-year and parsec	2
	how sunlight is absorbed and reflected	2

Lightning

Skill	Activity Suggestion	Foldable Parts
question	create a "know?-like to know? -learned" about lightning	3
investigate	different types of lightning: • cloud-to-cloud • cloud-to-air • cloud-to-ground • ground-to-cloud	4
	the percentage of lightning bolts that actually strike Earth's surface	any number
illustrate	forms of lightning, including forked, streak, ribbon, bead, sheet, or ball lightning	6
determine	regions that receive the most lightning strikes	1
research	the "who, what, when, where" of Benjamin Franklin	4
write	a lightning safety manual	any number

Liquids (Fluids)

Skill	Activity Suggestion	Foldable Parts
question	create a "know?-like to know? -learned" about liquids	3
describe	liquids as one of the four states of matter	4
observe	static fluids and fluids in motion	2
	and describe the movement of thin (water) and thick (syrup) liquids	2
make a concept map	showing gases and liquids as fluids	2
explain	how liquids can be changed by adding heat (raising temperature) or decreasing heat (lowering temperature)	2
	how the density of a liquid can be changed	1

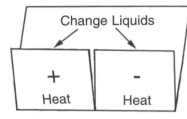

Two-tab concept map

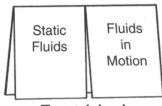

Two-tab book

Living Things

Skill	Activity Suggestion	Foldable Parts
question	create a "know?-like to know? -learned" about living organisms	3
explain	how living organisms are classified into Kingdoms	1
	producers, consumers, and decomposers	3
differentiate	between organic (living) and inorganic (nonliving) matter	2
compare and contrast	living organisms that produce their own food and those that depend upon other organisms for food	2
	living organisms in terrestrial and marine habitats	2
diagram	a cross-section of Earth's biosphere, including the parts of Earth above and below ground in which life exists	2
discuss	the statement "Every living organism changes Earth."	1
	the statement "Living organisms are matter and energy that use the matter and energy around them to survive."	1
list	pros and cons of one-celled life and many-celled life	2
	four things organisms need to survive and reproduce	4

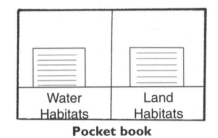

Pocket book

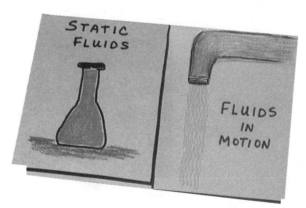

3x3 Folded chart

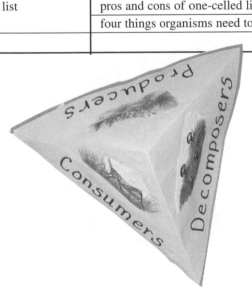

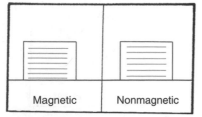

Magnetism

Skill	Activity Suggestion	Foldable Parts
question	create a "know?-like to know? -learned" about magnetism	3
compare	magnetic and nonmagnetic matter	2
	natural magnets and commercially produced magnets	2
design	an activity to show the following: • like poles repel • opposite poles attract • a magnet can be used to magnetize metal	3
diagram	a bar magnet placed in iron filings	1
explain	force of magnetism, including attraction and repulsion	2
research	the magnetic lines of force of Earth and draw them	2
make a time line	from the discovery of magnetite (loadstone) to the use of magnets in technology	any number
graph	thirty objects as either magnetic or nonmagnetic	2

Pocket book

Two-tab book

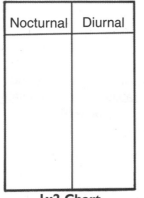

1x2 Chart

Mammals

Skill	Activity Suggestion	Foldable Parts
question	create a "know?-like to know? -learned" about mammals	3
compare and contrast	land and aquatic mammals	2
	reproduction in mammals bearing live young and the two mammals that lay eggs	2
	nocturnal and diurnal mammals	2
report on	monotremes, marsupials, and placental mammals	3
describe	two or more characteristics of mammals, including warm-blooded, fur or hair, females produce milk, and live birth	2+
list	threatened and endangered mammals	2
make a table	for five mammals, including size, diet, habitat, life span, and young	5

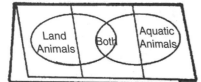

Three-tab Venn diagram

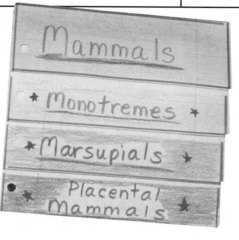

Matter

Skill	Activity Suggestion	Foldable Parts
question	create a "know?-like to know? -learned" about matter	3
define	matter, including that it occupies space and has weight	2
describe	the four states of matter: • solid • liquid • gas • plasma	4
chart	common examples of solids, liquids, and gases	3
list	examples of organic and inorganic matter	2
discuss	the statement "Everything in the known world is either matter or energy."	1
investigate	and report on matter and energy	2 .
identify	types of matter: • element— made of only one type of atom • compound— made of more than one type of atom	2
explain	how matter can be changed by adding or deleting heat	2

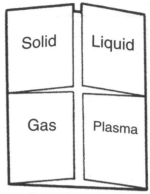

Four-door book

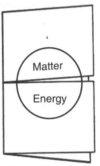

Two-tab book

Meteorites

Skill	Activity Suggestion	Foldable Parts
question	create a "know?-like to know? -learned" about meteors and meteorites	2
differentiate	between meteoroid, meteor, and meteorite	3
describe	shooting stars as meteors in Earth's atmosphere	1
predict	two things that would happen if a large meteorite impacted Earth's ocean	2
	two things that would happen if a large meteorite impacted Earth's land	2
research	the "who, what, when, where" of Daniel Barringer	4
	the "what, when, where, how" of the Ahnighito Meteorite	4
	myths or legends about meteors and meteorites	any number
graph	the sizes of the largest known meteorites	any number
locate on a map	famous meteorite craters worldwide	any number
name	three classifications of meteorites • stones • stony-irons • irons	3

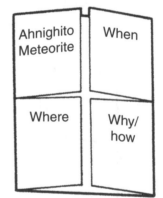

Four-door book

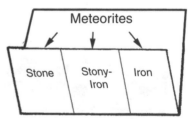

Three-tab concept map

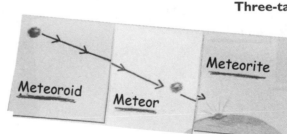

Motion

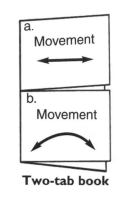

Laws of Motion

1st
2nd
3rd

**Layered-look book
(2 sheets of paper)**

Skill	Activity Suggestion	Foldable Parts
question	create a "know?-like to know? -learned" about motion	3
compare and contrast	rectilinear motion (objects move in straight lines) and curvilinear motion (objects move along a curved path)	2
describe	motion using the terms displacement, velocity, and acceleration	3
	how velocity and speed differ	2
	kinetic energy as the energy of motion	1
research	Isaac Newton's three laws of motion	3
	the "who, what, when, where" of Isaac Newton	4

a. Movement

b. Movement

Two-tab book

Ocean Exploration

Skill	Activity Suggestion	Foldable Parts
question	create a "know?-like to know? -learned" about ocean exploration	3
discuss	the statement "The ocean is Earth's last frontier."	1
make a model	of an early ocean-going vessel	1
make a time line	of oceanography as a science	any number
	of ocean surface exploration	any number
	of exploration of the ocean's depths	any number
investigate	past and present diving equipment	2
explain	three ways in which the world's oceans would be different today if humans had never existed	3
read	tales of ocean exploration	any number
sequence	events of the ship *Titanic* from the time it set sail to its discovery on the ocean floor	any number
research	the "what, where, when, why/how" of any of the following: • H.M.S. Challenger • Alvin • Ocean Drilling Project	4
	the "who, what, when, where" of any of the following: • Pytheas • Robert D. Ballard • Jacques-Yves Cousteau	
show cause and effect	of exploration by sea in the past and present, possibly including economics, search of new lands, trade routes, and spread of religion	2

Titanic
Report

Picture-frame book

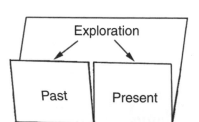

Exploration

Past   Present

Two-tab concept map

Who:
Isaac
Newton

What:
Laws of
Gravity and
Motion

When:
1642
to
1727

Where:
England

Ocean

Skill	Activity Suggestion	Foldable Parts
question	create a "know?-like to know? -learned" about oceanography	3
name	the world's oceans: • Atlantic Ocean • Pacific Ocean • Indian Ocean • Arctic Ocean	4
show	that Earth really has just one ocean since all oceans are connected	1
compare and contrast	the ocean biome and another biome	2
	the oceans by depth	2
	the oceans by surface area	2
	the oceans by number of islands and volcanoes	2
	seas, gulfs, and bays	3
debate	calling our planet "Earth" instead of "Ocean"	2
	the question "Who owns the ocean?"	1
graph	the percent of Earth's water 97% in the ocean, 2% frozen freshwater, and 1%liquid freshwater	3
identify	four major ocean resources, possibly including food, energy, minerals, medicines, and oil	4
illustrate	the water cycle, including evaporation, condensation, and precipitation	3
invent	methods for desalinating ocean water	any number
describe	two effects of global warming on the ocean's levels	2
research	changes in the ocean's shape through geologic time	any number
	the ocean's effect on climate and weather	2
	ocean ridges and ocean trenches	2
show cause and effect	of ocean pollution	2
	of noise pollution in the ocean	2
investigate	types of ocean sediments, including hydrogenous (sediments from water), biogenous (sediments from living organisms), and lithogenous (sediments from land)	3
make a model	of the ocean floor including four of the following: • ocean ridges or trenches • submarine volcanoes • seamounts and/or guyots • abyssal plains and/or abyssal hills	4
diagram	the continental margin, including shelf, slope, and continental rise	3
	the largest and longest ridges in each ocean on a map	2

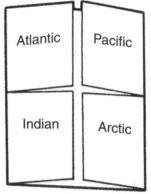

Ocean	Depth	Surface Area	Average Temp.
Atlantic			
Indian			
Pacific			

4x4 Folded chart

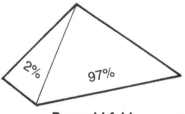

Four-door book

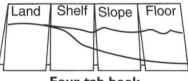

Pyramid fold

Four-tab book

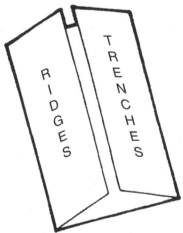

Shutter-fold book

Ocean	Depth	Surface Area	Number of Islands and Volcanoes	Average Temperature
Atlantic	12,900 ft.	31.8 million sq. miles		32°-81°F
Pacific	14,000 ft.	64 million sq. miles	25,000	
Indian	12,800 ft.	28.3 million sq. miles		
Arctic	5,450 ft.	5.4 million sq. miles		

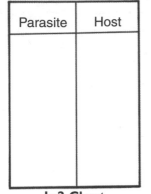

1x2 Chart

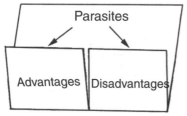

Two-tab concept map

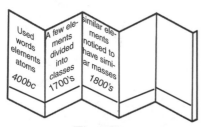

Time line:
History of the
Periodic Table of Elements

Matchbook

Parasites

Skill	Activity Suggestion	Foldable Parts
question	create a "know?-like to know? -learned" about parasites	3
list	parasites and their hosts	2
classify	Phylum Platyhelminthes:parasitic and nonparasitic • flatworms • planarians Phylum Nematoda: parasitic and nonparasitic • roundworms • hookworms • spinworms • trichinae • filariae Phylum Acanthocephala: parasitic and nonparasitic • acanthocephalan	3

Periodic Table of Elements

Skill	Activity Suggestion	Foldable Parts
question	create a "know?-like to know? -learned" about the Periodic Table of Elements	3
make a time line	of the history of the periodic table of elements	any number
make	giant periodic table and record information on each element under the tabs	1
explain	the information given for each element in the periodic table: • symbol for the element • atomic weight • atomic number	3

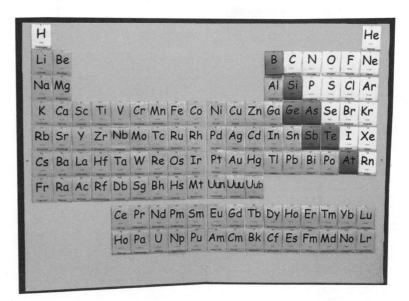

Planets

Skill	Activity Suggestion	Foldable Parts
question	create a "know?-like to know? -learned" about planets	3
compare and contrast	planets, stars, and satellites	3
	the inner planets and the outer planets	2
	solid planets and gaseous planets	2
	selected planets' rotation and revolution	2
	our solar system to another solar system	2
discuss	past and present views of the Sun's position in relation to the planets	2
diagram	the solar system	1
explain	two ways planets are affected by their distance from the Sun, including atmosphere and revolution period	2
collect	information on each of the nine planets	9
make a table	of information on the nine planets	9
make a model	of the inner planets: Mercury, Venus, Earth, Mars	4
	of the outer planets: Jupiter, Saturn, Uranus, Neptune, and Pluto	5
make a time line	of planet discoveries	any number
research	mythology as it relates to astronomy: • Apollo, the sun god • Diana, goddess of the moon • planets named after mythological gods and goddesses	any number
	planets with and without satellites	2
	the three most common elements in the Universe	3
	new solar system discoveries	any number
	the "who, what, when, where" of any of the following: • Hipparchus • Nicolaus Copernicus • Johannes Kepler • Johann Elert Bode • Pierre Simon de Laplace	4
	the "what, when, where, why/how" of any of the following: • Keck Observatory, Hawaii • National Radio Astronomy Observatory, New Mexico • McDonald Observatory, Texas • Arecibo Observatory, Puerto Rico	4

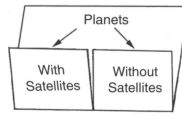

Two-tab concept map

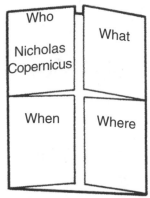

Four-door book

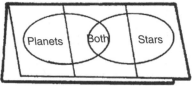

Three-tab Venn diagram

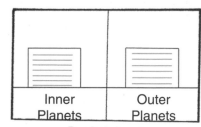

Pocket book

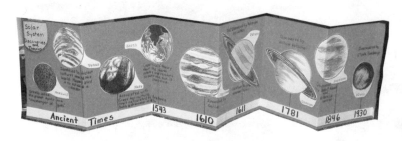

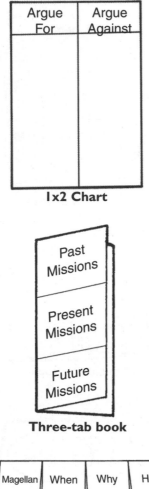

1x2 Chart

Three-tab book

Past Missions

Present Missions

Future Missions

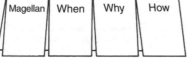

Magellan | When | Why | How

Four-tab book

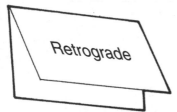

Retrograde

Half book

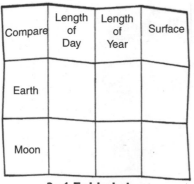

Compare	Length of Day	Length of Year	Surface
Earth			
Moon			

3x4 Folded chart

Planet: Mercury

Skill	Activity Suggestion	Foldable Parts
question	create a "know?-like to know? -learned" about Mercury	3
compare and contrast	Mercury and Earth	2
	Mercury's elliptical orbit in comparison to that of other planets	2
	cross sections of Mercury and Earth	2
argue	for and against sending missions to Mars	1
make a diorama	of the planet Mercury showing a cross section	1
explain	how to identify Mercury, including how it is visible at sunrise and sunset and stays low in the sky	2
	why Mercury is closer to the Sun, but Venus is hotter	2
illustrate	Mercury as part of the solar system	any number
research	how Mercury got its name	1
	past, present, and future Mercury missions	3
	the "what, where, when, why/how" of *Mariner 10*	4

Planet: Venus

Skill	Activity Suggestion	Foldable Parts
question	create a "know?-like to know? -learned" about Venus	3
compare and contrast	Venus' length of day and year to Earth's	2
	Mars and Venus	2
define	retrograde	1
diagram	the surface of Venus as revealed by the Magellan spacecraft	any number
explain	two ways to identify Venus, including how it shines bright in the sky and is noted for evening and morning appearances	2
	why the Sun rises in the west and sets in the east on Venus	2
research	the clouds covering Venus	1
	the "who, what, when, where" of Jeremiah Horrocks	4

Planet: Earth

Skill	Activity Suggestion	Foldable Parts
question	create a "know?-like to know? -learned" about Earth as a planet in the solar system	3
compare and contrast	Earth's atmosphere composition and that of other planets	2
	an Earth day to a day on another planet	2
	geologic features of Earth and those of another planet	2
describe	Earth as seen from space	1
	why the Sun rises in the east and sets in the West on Earth	2
identify	three things that make Earth unique from other planets	3
prove	the importance of liquid water to Earth	1

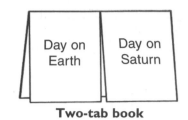

Two-tab book

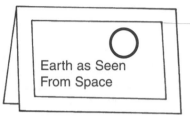

Picture-frame book

Planet: Mars

Skill	Activity Suggestion	Foldable Parts
question	create a "know?-like to know? -learned" about Mars	3
compare and	ancient and current views of Mars	2
contrast	a day and a year on Mars and Earth	2
diagram	the surface of Mars	1
explain	why humankind expected to find life on Mars	1
illustrate	Mars as part of the solar system	9
list	ways in which Mars and Earth are similar and different	2
make a table	including size, gravity and mass of Mars and Earth	3
make a Venn diagram	labeled *Phobos*, *Deimos*, and *both*	3
research	the "who, what, when, where" of any of the following: • Asaph Hall • Giovanni Viginio Schiaparell • Percival Lowell	4

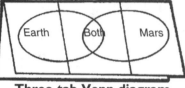

Three-tab Venn diagram

3x4 Folded chart

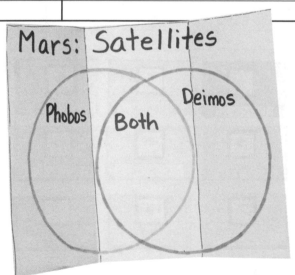

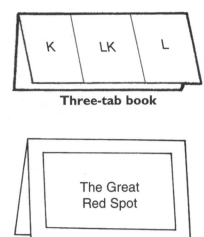

Three-tab book

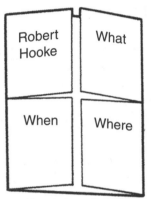

The Great
Red Spot

Picture-frame book

Robert
Hooke | What

When | Where

Four-door book

R
I
N
G
S | Cassini's
D
i
v
i
s
i
o
n | R
I
N
G
S

Trifold book

Planet: Jupiter

Skill	Activity Suggestion	Foldable Parts
question	create a "know?-like to know? -learned" about the planet Jupiter	3
describe	Jupiter as the largest gaseous planet and compare it to another gaseous planet	2
debate	sending a crewed mission to Jupiter	1
investigate	the weather of Jupiter and the Great Red Spot	2
illustrate	Jupiter as part of the solar system	9
list	three similarities between Jupiter and the other gaseous planets	3
make a table	including size, gravity, and mass of Jupiter and Earth	3
	of data pertaining to missions to observe Jupiter	any number
research	the ring that surrounds Jupiter and compare it to the rings surrounding another gaseous planet	2
	the "who, what, when, where" of Robert Hooke	4

Planet: Saturn

Skill	Activity Suggestion	Foldable Parts
question	create a "know?-like to know? -learned" about Saturn	3
compare and contrast	Saturn's length of day and year to Jupiter's	2
	Saturn's orbit to that of other planets	2
describe	the "what" and "where" of Cassini's Division	2
diagram	Saturn's rings	any number
explain	why Saturn and Jupiter produce more heat than they receive from the Sun	2
illustrate	Saturn as part of the solar system	9
make a table	including size, gravity, and mass of Saturn and Earth	3
make a time line	of observations and explorations of Saturn	any number
research	the most recent data on the composition of Saturn's rings	any number
	at least four of Saturn's moons	4
	the "who, what, when, where" of any of the following: • Giovanni Domenico Cassini • Christiaan Huygens • Johann Franz Encke	4

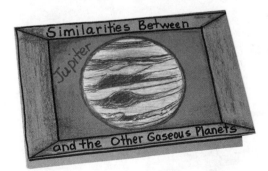

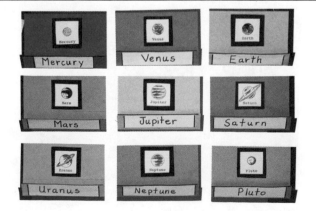

Planet: Uranus

Skill	Activity Suggestion	Foldable Parts
question	create a "know?-like to know? -learned" about Uranus	3
compare and contrast	Uranus's length of day and year to Saturn's	2
	Uranus's orbit to that of another planet	2
	Uranus and other gaseous planets	2
	Uranus's moon Miranda to Earth's Moon	2
explain	how the discovery of Uranus doubled the known solar system's size	1
make a table	showing the size, gravity, and mass of Uranus and Earth	3
make a time line	of observations and discoveries of Uranus	2
research	the discovery of Uranus	1
	new information learned from the *Voyager* journeys	any number
	the "who, what, when, where" of William Hershet	4

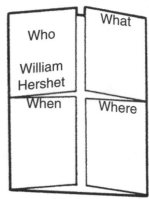

Three-tab Venn diagram

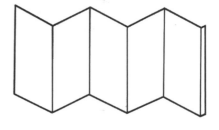

Four-door book

Planet: Neptune

Skill	Activity Suggestion	Foldable Parts
question	create a "know?-like to know? -learned" about Neptune	3
chart	information concerning Neptune's moons	any number
compare and contrast	Neptune's length of day and year to Uranus's	2
	Neptune's moon Triton to Earth's moon	2
diagram	the five barely visible rings that surround Neptune and compare them to Saturn's rings	2
explain	why Neptune looks blue	1
illustrate	Neptune as part of the solar system	9
make a table	including size, gravity, and mass of Neptune and Earth	3
make a time line	of Neptune observations and discoveries	any number
research	the Great Dark Spot	1
	the "who, what, when, where" of any of the following: • Urbain Jean Leverrier • Johann G. Galle • John Couch Adams	4

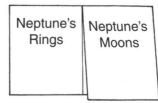

**Time line:
of Neptune Observations
and Discoveries**

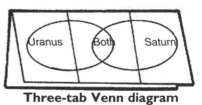

Three-quarter book

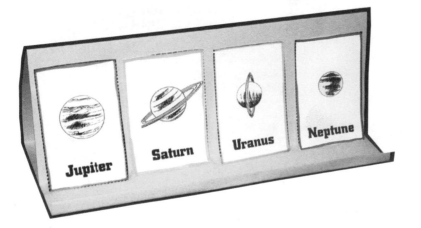

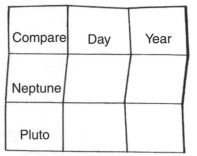

Compare	Day	Year
Neptune		
Pluto		

3x3 Folded chart

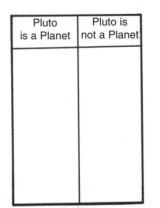

Pluto is a Planet	Pluto is not a Planet

1x2 Chart

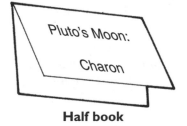

Pluto's Moon:

Charon

Half book

Planet: Pluto

Skill	Activity Suggestion	Foldable Parts
question	create a "know?-like to know? -learned" about Pluto	3
compare and contrast	Pluto's orbit to that of other planets	any number
	Pluto's length of day and year to Neptune's	2
debate	whether Pluto is or is not a planet	2
explain	how Pluto got its name	1
make a table	of data pertaining to missions to observe Pluto	any number
make a time line	of observations and discoveries of Pluto	2
research	Pluto's atmospheric conditions	1
	the "what" and "where" of Pluto's moon, Charon	2
	the controversy over Pluto's classification	1
	the "who, what, when, where" of: • Peercival Lowell • Clyde Tombaugh	4

Plants

Skill	Activity Suggestion	Foldable Parts
question	create a "know?-like to know? -learned" about plants	3
differentiate	between vascular and nonvascular plants	2
compare and contrast	land and water plants	2
	positive and negative tropisms	2
	day-flowering plants and night-flowering plants	2
describe	three of the basic groups of plants: • seed plants • ferns • lycophytes • horsetails • bryophytes	3
	the scientific classification of plants into divisions	10
diagram	plant respiration	any number
	vascular tissue, including xylem and phloem	2
	the parts of a flowering plant	any number
explain	the structure of a plant cell and compare it to an animal cell	2
	the importance of cellulose for support and retention of water	2
	the importance of chloroplasts and chlorophyll	2
graph	some of the world's largest plants, living or extinct	any number
	some of the world's smallest plants, living or extinct	any number
	average life span of selected plants	any number
illustrate	a plant cell and label the parts	any number
list	advantages and disadvantages of plants living on land	2
make a Venn diagram	labeled animal cell, plant cell, and both	3
	labeled seed plants, seedless plants, and both	3
observe	a plant with a cuticle	1
	perennial and annual plants	2
outline	the movement of water through a plant	any number
research	fossil evidence of plants	1
	three characteristics of plants	3
	how plants get food, including autotrophs and heterotrophs	2
	plants with chlorophyll and plants with little or no chlorophyll	2
	three carnivorous (insect-eating) plants	3
	the "who, what, when, where" of any of the following: Carolus Linnaeus, Gregor Mendel, or Barbara McClintock	4
show cause and effect	of transpiration	2
summarize	the process of photosynthesis	any number
	the importance of plants in our daily lives	any number

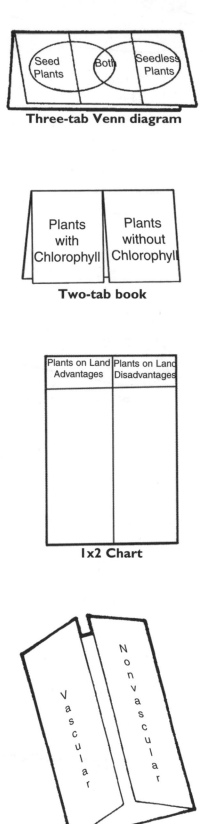

Three-tab Venn diagram

Two-tab book

1x2 Chart

Shutter-fold book

Plant Cell

Precipitation

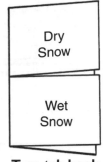

Two-tab book

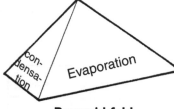

Pyramid fold

Skill	Activity Suggestion	Foldable Parts
question	create a "know?-like to know? -learned" about precipitation	3
describe	four types of precipitation: • rain • snow • hail • sleet	4
	the formation of hailstones	1
design	six-sided paper snow crystals and describe them	2
diagram	the water cycle, including evaporation, condensation, and precipitation	3
	a rainbow (spectrum)	7
measure and record	precipitation amounts over a given period of time	any number
graph	precipitation amounts over a given period of time	any number
compare	actual raindrop shape and perceived shape	2
	regions of Earth that receive high and low levels of precipitation	2
	hail and sleet	2
	dry snow and wet snow	2
research	how tree rings can help determine past rainfall amounts	1

Protists

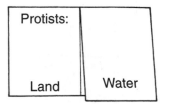

Three-quarter book

Skill	Activity Suggestion	Foldable Parts
question	create a "know?-like to know? -learned" about protists	3
describe	protists that live in water and protists that live on land	2
compare	protists that are microscopic to those that are visible	2
	the Protist Kingdom to the Plant Kingdom	2
research	the "what" and "where" of seaweed	2
report on	three or more of the following Protists: • green algae • slime molds • diatoms • dinoflagellates • euglenas	3+
explain	two characteristics all protists have in common: • nucleus= eukaryotic single or many-celled organism • live in damp environments	2

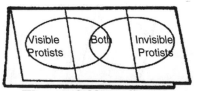

Three-tab Venn diagram

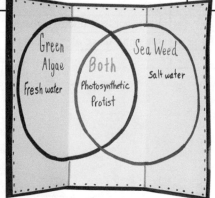

Rainbows

Skill	Activity Suggestion	Foldable Parts
question	create a "know?-like to know? -learned" about rainbows	3
draw and color	a rainbow	1
describe	a rainbow as a spectrum: red, orange, yellow, green, blue, indigo, and violet	7
explain	two conditions needed for a rainbow to form: • sunlight • moisture in the air	2
make	a rainbow by standing with your back to the Sun and spraying water into the air	1
investigate	myths and legends relating to rainbows	any number
determine	if rainbows really do have an "end" where a pot of gold could be hidden	1

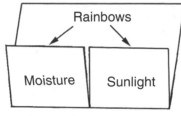

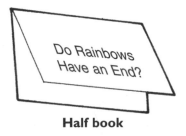

Two-tab concept map

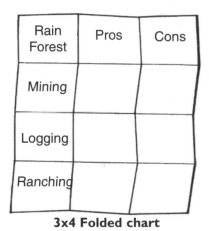

Half book

Rain Forest

Skill	Activity Suggestion	Foldable Parts
question	create a "know?-like to know? -learned" about rain forests	3
compare and contrast	a rain forest and a deciduous forest biome	2
	the inner and outer regions of a rain forest	2
debate	pros and cons of mining in rain forests	2
	pros and cons of logging in rain forests	2
	pros and cons of clearing rain forests to raise cattle	2
describe	a rain forest, including rainfall amount, temperature averages, vegetation, and humidity	4
diagram	and label the layers of a rain forest: • emergent layer • canopy • understory • shrub layer • herb layer	5
explain	plants and animals common to a specific rain forest	2
summarize	the importance of rain forests	1
research	rain forests in South America, Africa, and Asia	3

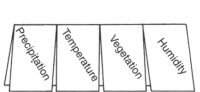

3x4 Folded chart

Four-tab book

Reptiles

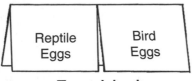

Two-tab book

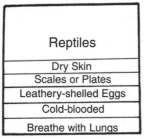

3x4 Folded chart

Skill	Activity Suggestion	Foldable Parts
question	create a "know?-like to know? -learned" about reptiles	3
compare and contrast	reptiles that do and do not hibernate	2
	lizards with and without legs	2
	lizards and snakes	2
	turtles and tortoises	2
	reptile eggs and bird eggs	2
	living and extinct reptiles	2
create	a reptile identification chart	1
describe	three or more characteristics of reptiles: • dry skin • scales or bony plates • leathery-shelled eggs • breathe with lungs • cold-blooded	3
make a table	comparing the characteristics of snakes, lizards, turtles, and crocodilians	4
explain	the importance of molting to reptiles	1
research	poisonous and nonpoisonous reptiles	2

**Layered-look book
(3 sheets of paper)**

Four-tab book

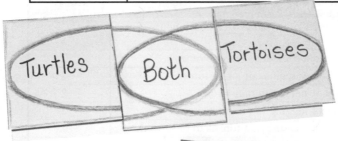

Rocks

Skill	Activity Suggestion	Foldable Parts
question	create a "know?-like to know? -learned" about rocks	3
chart	examples of igneous, metamorphic, and sedimentary rocks	3
compare and contrast	foliated and nonfoliated metamorphic rocks	2
	igneous, metamorphic, and sedimentary rocks	3
	detrital, chemical, and organic sedimentary rocks	3
explain	why the rock cycle has more than one path	1
	why nearly all fossils are found in sedimentary rocks	1
make a Venn diagram	labeled rocks, minerals, and both	3
	labeled marine sedimentary rock, terrestrial sedimentary rock, and both	3
research	extrusive and intrusive igneous rocks	2
	the "what, where, when, why/how" of the idea of uniformitarianism	4

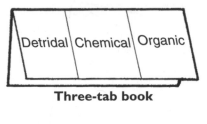

Three-tab book

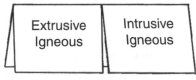

Two-tab book

Roots

Skill	Activity Suggestion	Foldable Parts
question	create a "know?-like to know? -learned" about roots	3
compare and contrast	primary roots and secondary roots	2
	roots found in soil, water, and air	3
	prop roots, aerial roots, and below-ground root systems	3
describe	the form and function of primary root, secondary root, root cap, and root hairs	4
	three purposes of roots, including anchor, collecting nutrients from soil, and collecting water	3
diagram	a fibrous root system and a taproot system	2
explain	how and why some roots act as a storage area for food	2
	how roots help prevent soil erosion	1
research	two of the following: cassava, banyan tree, legumes, chicory, licorice, sugar beets, peanuts, horseradish	2

**Layered-look book
(2 sheets of paper)**

3x3 Folded chart

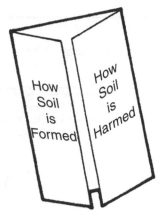

Shutter-fold book

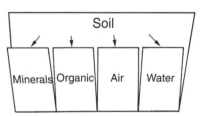

Four-tab concept map

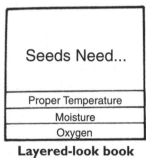

**Layered-look book
(2 sheets of paper)**

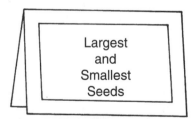

Picture-frame book

Sand and Soil

Skill	Activity Suggestion	Foldable Parts
question	create a "know?-like to know? -learned" about sand and soil	3
make a Venn	labeled *sand*, *soil*, and *both*	3
diagram	labeled *humus*, *soil*, and *both*	3
explain	how soils are formed and destroyed	2
compare	sands, silts, and clays	3
describe	the formation of sand and the formation of soil	2
observe	soil characteristics, including color, composition, and location	3
list	soil contents, including minerals, organic matter, air, and water	4
research	three soil organisms	3
	farming techniques that do and do not result in the erosion of top soil	2

Seeds

Skill	Activity Suggestion	Foldable Parts
question	create a "know?-like to know? -learned" about seeds	3
collect	different seeds and sketch or trace around them	2
compare and contrast	types of seed plants, including flowering and nonflowering	2
	largest and smallest seeds	2
	seed development in angiosperms and gymnosperms	2
describe	four ways in which seeds are dispersed • wind • water • animal • explosion	4
diagram	parts of a seed and parts of a seedling	2
	monocotyledons and dicotyledons	2
chart	examples of monocot and dicot seeds	2
research	common and uncommon uses of seeds	2
outline	three needs of seeds to grow, including proper temperature, moisture, and oxygen	3

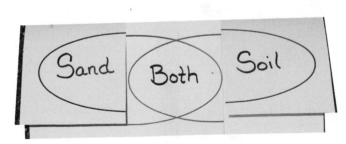

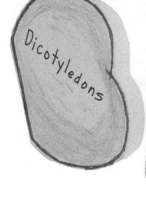

Senses: Sight

Skill	Activity Suggestion	Foldable Parts
question	create a "know?-like to know? -learned" about eyes	3
diagram	the human eye, including cornea, iris, pupil, lens, retina, and optic nerve	6
compare and contrast	the human eye to an insect eye	2
	near-sighted vision and far-sighted vision	2
	a human eyelid to a bird's eyelid	2
explain	the use of convex and concave lenses to correct vision	2
graph	sizes of different eyes	any number
identify	problems and solutions to vision requirements of animals living in total darkness	2
illustrate	the visible parts of the eye, including white and iris	2
research	purposes of the dilator muscle and sphincter muscle	2

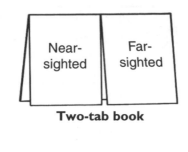

Two-tab book

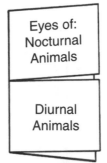

Two-tab book

Senses: Touch

Skill	Activity Suggestion	Foldable Parts
question	create a "know?-like to know? -learned" about the sense of touch	3
describe	three or more purposes of skin, including preventing fluid loss, defense against disease, protection from the sun, protection from harmful substances, and regulation of body temperature	3+
	skin as the largest organ	1
investigate	the form and function of sweat glands and sweat	2
diagram	the layers of human skin, including epidermis, dermis, and subcutaneous tissue	3
explain	the cause and effect of melanin in skin	2
	dandruff as the scalp shedding skin	1
research	skin color, freckles, and age spots	3
	how frequently human skin is shed and replaced	2

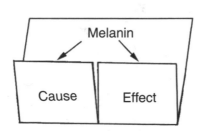

Two-tab concept map

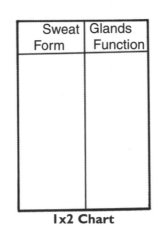

1x2 Chart

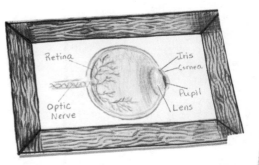

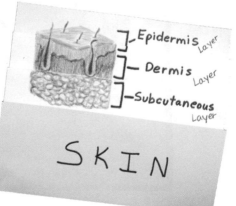

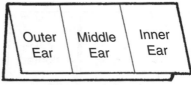

Three-tab book

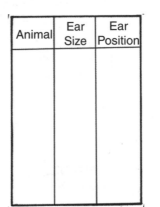

1x3 Chart

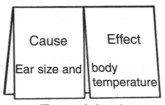

Two-tab book

Four-tab book

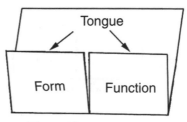

Two-tab concept map

Senses: Hearing

Skill	Activity Suggestion	Foldable Parts
question	create a "know?-like to know? -learned" about ears and the sense of hearing	3
diagram	the human ear, including inner ear, middle ear, and outer ear	3
	each of the following: • inner ear • middle ear • outer ear	3
list	animals with and without ears	2
discuss	problems and solutions for hearing needs of animals with poor eyesight	2
make a chart	of different animals, their ear positions, and ear size	any number
show cause and effect	of size of ear lobe for retaining and losing heat, possibly looking at elephants, polar bears, fennec fox, jackrabbits, others	any number

Senses: Taste

Skill	Activity Suggestion	Foldable Parts
question	create a "know?-like to know? -learned" about the mouth, tongue, and the sense of taste	3
compare and contrast	kinds of taste, possibly including sour, sweet, salty, and bitter	2+
design an experiment	to test the areas of taste on the human tongue	1
diagram	a taste bud	any number
explain	how taste and smell are related	2
sequence	what happens internally when something is tasted	any number
describe	form and function of the tongue of two different animals, including information on applicable things such as taste, moving food, speech or calls, catching food, lapping, cleaning fur, others	2

Animal	Tongue	Use / Purpose
	thick, black, tough, very long, up to 20 inches	grasping food, lapping water
	pink color	cleaning fur, lapping water, moving food, making sounds
	forked	smells food, finds prey with it
	sticky	catching food, making sounds
	long, thin, moves fast	catching food

Senses: Smell

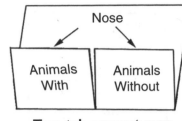

Nose

Animals With / Animals Without

Two-tab concept map

Skill	Activity Suggestion	Foldable Parts
question	create a "know?-like to know? -learned" about the nose and the sense of smell	3
compare and contrast	animals with and without a nose	2
	animals with a strong sense of smell, animals with an underdeveloped sense of smell, and animals with no sense of smell	3
describe	nose purposes, including breathing, smelling, and moisturizing air moving into lungs	3
diagram	the path of breath of air, including nostrils, nasal passages, pharynx, trachea, and lungs	5
graph	sizes of different animal noses	any number
make a chart	of different animals, their nose positions, nose size, dependence upon their sense of smell, others	any number
sequence	the internal and external events that are associated with the sense of smell, including olfactory nerve receptors, olfactory nerve fibers, and the olfactory bulb in the brain	any number
show cause and effect	of the sense of smell as it relates to taste	2
research	two animals with unusual noses, possibly including elephants and/or proboscis monkeys	2
explain	the relationship between the sense of smell and taste	2

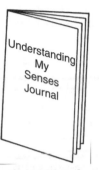

Understanding My Senses Journal

Bound book

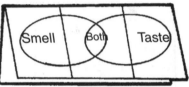

Smell / Both / Taste

Three-tab Venn diagram

Five Senses

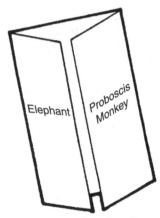

Elephant / Proboscis Monkey

Shutter-fold book

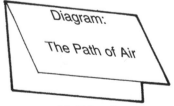

Diagram: The Path of Air

Half book

Simple Tools, Machines, and Work

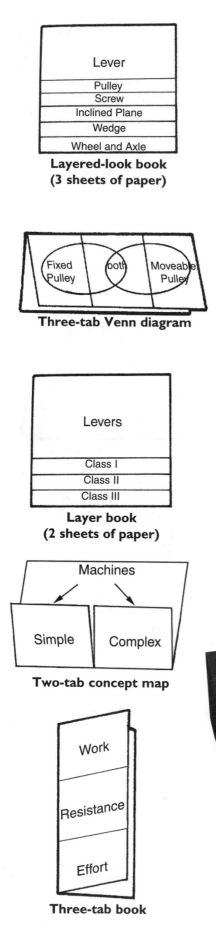

Lever
Pulley
Screw
Inclined Plane
Wedge
Wheel and Axle

Layered-look book
(3 sheets of paper)

Fixed Pulley | both | Moveable Pulley

Three-tab Venn diagram

Levers
Class I
Class II
Class III

Layer book
(2 sheets of paper)

Machines
Simple | Complex

Two-tab concept map

Work
Resistance
Effort

Three-tab book

Skill	Activity Suggestion	Foldable Parts
question	create a "know?-like to know? -learned" about simple tools and machines	3
describe	the six simple machines and give examples of each: • lever • pulley • screw • inclined plane • wedge • wheel-and-axle	6
	a wheel and axle as a lever and show examples	any number
	the function of a wedge	1
compare and contrast	a fixed pulley and a moveable pulley	2
	a screw and a spiral staircase	2
	simple machines and compound machines	2
diagram	a lever as a rigid bar resting on a fixed point, or fulcrum	2
explain	the statement "If you push a rock and it doesn't move, work has not been done."	1
illustrate	the thread and pitch of a screw	2
	three classes of levers, including the following: • 1st class—fulcrum between effort force and resistance • 2nd class--resistance force in middle, effort and resistance force at ends • 3rd class--effort force between the resistance force and fulcrum	3
make a time line	of inventions and technology	any number
show cause and effect	of friction as it relates to machines	2
write	about situations in which levers perform work	any number
research	the "who, what, when, where" of Archimedes, Leonardo Da Vinci, James Watt, others	4
define	effort and resistance as they relate to tools	2
	work as a force used times distance moved	1

Solids

Skill	Activity Suggestion	Foldable Parts
question	create a "know?-like to know? -learned" about solids	3
list	five examples of solids	5
describe	solids as one of the four states of matter	4
	how four solids occupy space and have weight	4
	the characteristics of solids: • definite size • definite shape	2
compare and contrast	solids and liquids	2
	solids and gases	2
Venn diagram	of two solids and determine what they both have in common	3

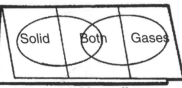

Three-tab Venn diagram

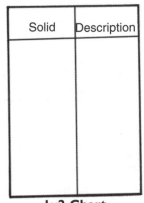

1x2 Chart

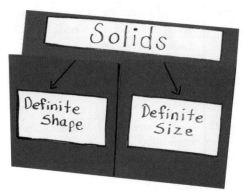

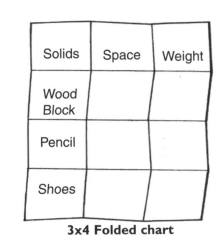

3x4 Folded chart

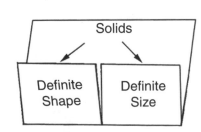

Two-tab concept map

Sound

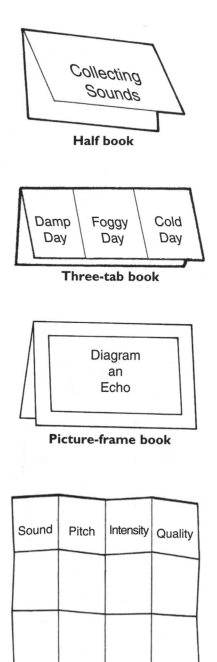

Half book

Collecting Sounds

Three-tab book

Damp Day | Foggy Day | Cold Day

Picture-frame book

Diagram an Echo

3x4 Folded chart

Sound | Pitch | Intensity | Quality

Skill	Activity Suggestion	Foldable Parts
question	create a "know?-like to know? -learned" about sound	3
list	all the sounds you hear in one minute, two minutes	2
explain	sound as a disturbance in the air, or some other "elastic medium" caused by vibration or shock	1
	the statement "Sound can be heard better and farther on damp, foggy, or cold days."	3
compare and contrast	pitch and frequency	2
	sound moving through warm air and cold air	2
	sound movement through liquids and gases	2
	sound movement through solids and liquids	2
	the speed of sound and the speed of light	2
describe	ultrasound and its uses	2
design an experiment	to show what types of matter sound travels through, including liquids, solids, and gases	3
diagram	an echo	1
discuss	"Sound cannot travel in a vacuum."	1
graph	decibels of common sounds	any number
illustrate	a sound wave	2
	the human ear as a sound receiver	any number
make a table	for the decibels of common sounds: • 10-20 decibels whispering • 60 decibels loud talking	any number
research	how sound moves by traveling in waves that move in all directions	1
	ways in which sounds differ in pitch, intensity, and quality	3
	the "who, what, when, where" of the following: • Christian Johann Doppler • Marin Mersenn • Ernst Mach • Charles E. Yeager	4
show cause and effect	of sound and animal survival	2

Stars

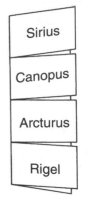

Four-tab book

Skill	Activity Suggestion	Foldable Part
question	create a "know?-like to know? -learned" about stars	3
observe	stars on a clear night and record your observations	2
describe	the Sun in our solar system as a star and sketch its location within the solar system	2
research	how stars produce energy	any number
	four of the brightest stars observed, possibly including Sirius, Canopus, Arcturus, Rigel, Vega, Polllux, Procyon, Regulus, or Stella	4
	Sirius, the brightest star in our night sky, and its importance to ancient Egypt	1
	the North Star's use for navigation in the northern hemisphere in the past and present	2
	the "who, what, when, where" of any of the following: • Jipparchus • Johann Bayer • Edward Emerson Barnard • Annie Jump Cannon • Henrietta Leavitt • Cecilia Payne-Gaposchkin • Hans Albrecht Bethe • Margaret Burbidge	4
describe	the composition of constellations	1
sketch	three constellations and describe their names	2
sequence	six stars from the closest to most distant, possibly including the Sun, Proxima Centauri, Alpha Centauri, Bernard's star, Wolf 359, Lalande 21185, Luyten 726-8A and 726-8B, Sirius A, Sirius B, and Ross 154	6
outline	the life of a star	any number
list	examples of absolute magnitudes from brightest to least bright stars	any number
explain	the significance of star spectra, including O, B, A, F, G, K, and M	any number
	two ways stars are documented, including numbered catalog identifications and names	2
	why there are only 88 constellations	1
diagram	sizes of stars: supergiants, red giants, blue main-sequence stars, medium-sized stars, white dwarfs, neutron stars, yellow dwarf, red dwarf, and black dwarf	8
	the cross-section of a typical star	any number
	binary stars and star clusters	2
compare and contrast	star colors and temperatures	2
	novas and supernovas	2
	apparent magnitude and absolute magnitude	2
	constellations and asterisms	2

Two-tab book

Past | Present

Picture-frame book

North Star

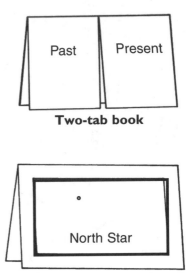

Star Spectra
o
b
a
f
g
k
m

Layered-look book (4 sheets of paper)

Star Colors | Star Temperatures

Compare and Contrast

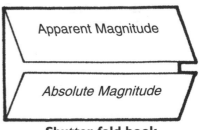

Apparent Magnitude

Absolute Magnitude

Shutter-fold book

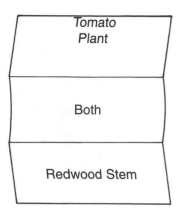

Tomato
Plant

Both

Redwood Stem

Trifold book

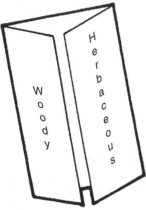

Woody

Herbaceous

Shutter-fold book

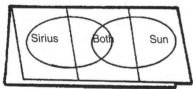

Sirius   Both   Sun

Three-tab Venn diagram

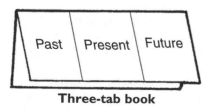

Past | Present | Future

Three-tab book

Stems

Skill	Activity Suggestion	Foldable Parts
question	create a "know?-like to know? -learned" about stems	3
observe	stems and record your observations	2
compare and contrast	plants with and without stems	2
	trunks, limbs, stems, and twigs	4
	a tomato plant stem to a redwood tree trunk	2
	human use of stems to that of other animals	2
	bulbs and tubers	2
define	stems in terms of transport and support	2
describe	petrified forests	1
illustrate	aerial and subterranean stems	2
list	examples of plants with woody stems and herbaceous stems	2
research	and describe four functions of a stem	4

Sun

Skill	Activity Suggestion	Foldable Parts
question	create a "know?-like to know? -learned" about the Sun	3
compare	the Sun to another star	2
compare and contrast	rotation and revolution	2
	theories of a Sun-centered solar system and an Earth-centered solar system through history	2
	the sizes of Earth and the Sun	2
	the use of solar energy to energy produced by fossil fuels	2
	solar energy use in the past and present	2
describe	why the Sun appears to rise and set	2
	the importance of the Sun as a source of energy, including how it gives Earth sunlight, moonlight, photosynthesis, weather patterns, the water cycle, and wind	any number
diagram	a cross-section of the Sun	any number
explain	the Sun's role in Earth's four seasonal changes	4
	moonlight as reflected sunlight	1
	how leaves are food factories powered by the Sun	1
make a time line	of Sun discoveries	any number
predict	future uses of solar energy	any number
research	the time it takes the Sun's light to reach Earth	1
	the causes and effects of sunspot cycles	2
	solar winds and solar flares	2
	myths and folklore pertaining to the Sun	any number
make a model	of the Sun	

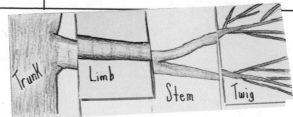

Systems of the Human Body

Skill	Activity Suggestion	Foldable Parts
question	create a "know?-like to know? -learned" about the systems of the human body	3
investigate	the following systems of the human body: • circulatory system • excretory system • digestive system • endocrine system • integumentary system (skin) • muscular system • nervous system • lymphatic system • reproductive system • respiratory system • skeletal system	11
explain	how the following systems are interdependent: • muscular and skeletal • digestive and excretory • circulatory and respiratory	2 2 2

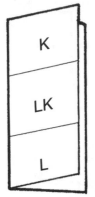

Three-tab book

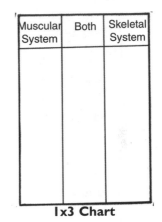

1x3 Chart

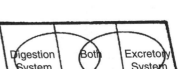
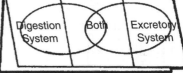

Three-tab Venn diagram

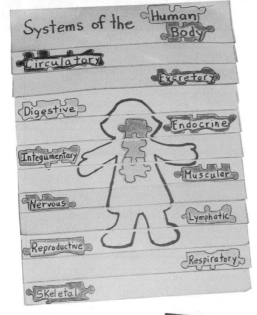

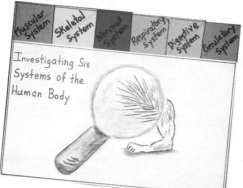

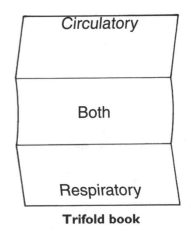

Trifold book

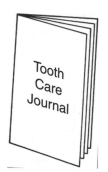

Animals	Teeth	Purpose
Sharks		
Horses		
Rodents		

3x4 Folded chart

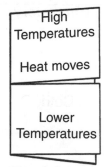

Tooth
Care
Journal

Bound book

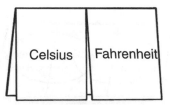

Celsius | Fahrenheit

Two-tab book

High
Temperatures

Heat moves

Lower
Temperatures

Two-tab book

Teeth

Skill	Activity Suggestion	Foldable Parts
question	create a "know?-like to know? -learned" about teeth	3
observe	your teeth and sketch what you observe	2
describe	the form and function of teeth	2
	why chewing is important to good digestion	1
make a Venn diagram	comparing "baby teeth", permanent teeth, and both	3
investigate	three animals and their teeth, possibly include sharks, elephants, horses, rodents, others	3
write	a pamphlet explaining how to properly care for teeth	1
research	four animals that use their teeth for defense	4

Temperature

Skill	Activity Suggestion	Foldable Parts
question	create a "know?-like to know? -learned" about temperature	3
compare and contrast	Celsius and Fahrenheit temperature scales	2
explain	boiling and freezing as they relate to temperature	2
	the need for measuring temperature using Kelvin	1
illustrate	heat transfer, which is energy moving from places with high temperatures to places with lower temperatures	2
describe	how warm-blooded animals and cold-blooded animals maintain a steady body temperature	2
record	your body temperature every hour for five hours and explain your data	2

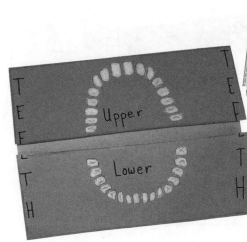

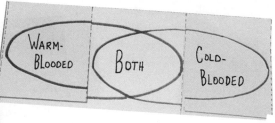

Thunder

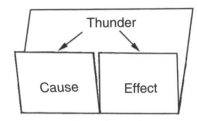

Skill	Activity Suggestion	Foldable Parts
question	create a "know?-like to know? -learned" about thunder	3
explain	the relationship between thunder and lightning	2
	the cause and effect of thunder	2
	how thunder and lightning can be used to roughly determine the distance of a thunderstorm	1
describe	what happens in a thunderstorm	any number
sketch	clouds that typically result in a thunderstorm	any number
research	myths and legends explaining thunder	any number

Two-tab concept map

Bound book

Tongue

Skill	Activity Suggestion	Foldable Parts
question	create a "know?-like to know? -learned" about your tongue	3
observe	your tongue and sketch what you see	2
diagram	a taste bud	any number
describe	the form and function of the human tongue	2
	how the tongue does each of the following: allows one to taste food, move food around in the mouth, and aids speech	3
	the purpose of papillae on the surface of the tongue	1
determine	why it is important to brush and clean the tongue as well as teeth	1
research	animals that use their tongues to catch food, clean their bodies, and sense the environment around them	3

Picture-frame book

1x3 Chart

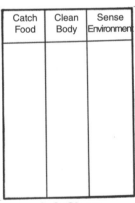

Tornadoes

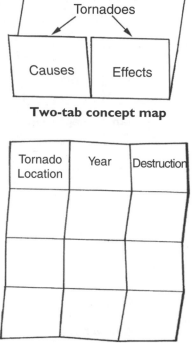

Two-tab concept map

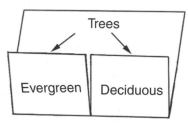

3x4 Folded chart

Skill	Activity Suggestion	Foldable Parts
question	create a "know?-like to know? -learned" about tornadoes	3
locate and describe	the area called "Tornado Alley" on a map	2
graph	the percentages of tornadoes occurring in different regions of the United States	2
diagram	a tornado and label the parts	any number
research	the causes and effects of tornadoes	2
design	a structure that would be resistant to tornado damage	1
compare and contrast	a tornado and a hurricane	2

Trees

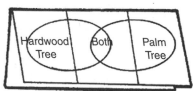

Two-tab concept map

Three-tab Venn diagram

Skill	Activity Suggestion	Foldable Parts
question	create a "know?-like to know? -learned" about trees	3
observe	a tree and describe what you observe	2
sketch	five different trees and describe the leaves, bark, and location of each	5
make	bark rubbings of three different trees and compare	3
diagram	the cross-section of a tree	any number
make a Venn diagram	of a hardwood tree, a palm tree, and tell what they both have in common	3
research	two of the largest species of trees on Earth	2
	the "what, when, where, why" of Arbor Day	4
list	ten products derived from trees	10
explain	trees as renewable resources	1
compare	past and present forest management practices	2
design	a poster that explains how to protect trees	1

Tsunami

Skill	Activity Suggestion	Foldable Parts
question	create a "know?-like to know? -learned" about tsunamis	3
explain	the causes and effects of a tsunami	2
describe	an imaginary town before and after a tsunami	2
research	historic and recent tsunamis	2
make a Venn Diagram	comparing a tidal wave, a tsunami, and both	3
locate on a map	geographic areas that are prone to tsunamis	any number
sequence	the events that lead up to a tsunami	any number
diagram	a tsunami—beginning, progressing, and ending	3

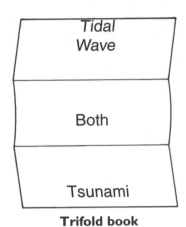

Trifold book

Shutter-fold book

Tundra

Skill	Activity Suggestion	Foldable Parts
question	create a "know?-like to know? -learned" about tundras	3
locate on a map	label and color all tundra biomes	1
	the Arctic tundra regions, including Alaska, Canada, Greenland, Iceland, Russia, and Scandinavia	6
compare and contrast	arctic tundra and alpine tundra, including information on weather, plants, and animals	2
	species diversity of the tundra and another biome	2
debate	mining or drilling for oil in tundra regions	2
describe	the rate at which tundra plants grow	1
diagram	tundra soil layers, including active surface soil and permafrost	2
research	people of the tundra past and present	2
	three or more tundra plants, including mosses, lichens, sedges, shrubs, buttercups, poppies, or willows	3

Tundra

Weather
Plants
Animals

**Layered-look book
(2 sheets of paper)**

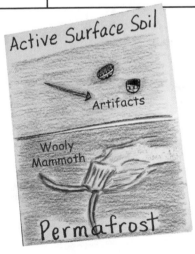

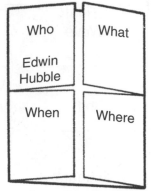

Four-door book

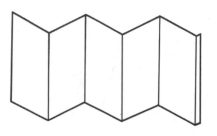

**Time line:
Discoveries about the Universe**

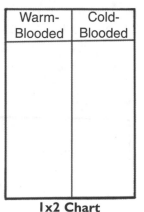

1x2 Chart

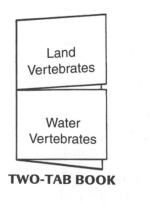

TWO-TAB BOOK

Universe

Skill	Activity Suggestion	Foldable Parts
question	create a "know?-like to know? -learned" about the universe	3
debate	whether the universe is infinite or finite	2
describe	views on the universe in the past and present	2
make a concept map	including universe, galaxy superclusters, galaxy clusters, galaxies, stars	5
make a time line	for discoveries relating to our understanding of the universe	any number
research	how astronomers learn about a galaxy	any number
	the "what, where, when, why/how" of the Andromeda galaxy	4
	the "who, what, where, when" of any of the following people: • Harlow Shapley • Edwin Powell Hubble • Stephen William Hawkings	4

Vertebrates

Skill	Activity Suggestion	Foldable Parts
question	create a "know?-like to know? -learned" about vertebrates	3
make a Venn diagram	comparing vertebrates, invertebrates, and both	3
list	examples of five vertebrates and describe each	5
	examples of land vertebrates and water vertebrates	2
research	the form and function of bone	2
explain	the advantages and disadvantages of internal skeletons	2
prove	that vertebrates are bilaterally symmetrical	1
chart	the seven classes of vertebrates, including three classes of fish, amphibians, reptiles, birds, mammals	7
compare	vertebrates that are endotherms and ectotherms	2

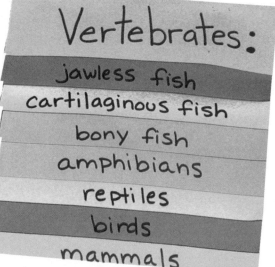

Volcanoes

Skill	Activity Suggestion	Foldable Parts
question	create a "know?-like to know? -learned" about volcanoes	3
compare	lava and magma	2
	a recent and historic volcanic eruption	2
	a crater and a caldera	2
explain	how the Hawaiian Islands formed	1
describe	an imaginary location before and after a volcanic eruption	2
	subduction zone volcanoes, rift volcanoes, and hot spot volcanoes	3
diagram	the Ring of Fire and explain its location on a map	2
	a cross-section of a volcano and label	any number
illustrate	classification of volcanic activity, including active, intermittent, dormant, and extinct	4
	the four types of volcanic eruptions	4
make a model	of a specific volcano, possibly Mt. St. Helens or Pinatubo	1
make a time line	of major volcanic eruptions worldwide	any number
make a table	pertaining to volcanoes and eruptions	any number
research	past and present volcanic activity on Iceland and Hawaii and predict future activity	2
sequence	events of a modern volcanic eruption	any number
show cause and effect	of Kilauea''s past and recent eruptions	2
	of volcanic activity and climate changes	2
sort	volcanoes into volcano groups, including shield, cinder, and composite	3
locate on a map	active volcanoes worldwide	any number
compare	explosive and gradual geologic changes	2

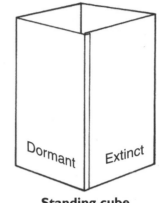

Standing cube

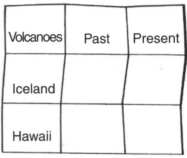

3x3 Folded chart

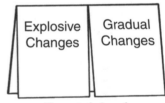

Two-tab book

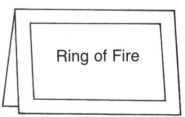

Picture-frame book

Water

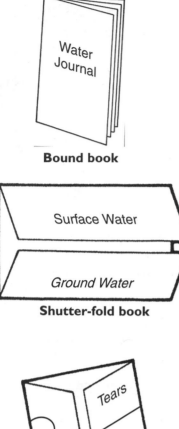

Bound book

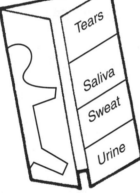

Shutter-fold book

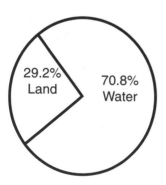

Shutter-fold book

Skill	Activity Suggestion	Foldable Parts
question	create a "know?-like to know? -learned" about water	3
compare and contrast	surface water and groundwater	2
	freshwater and salt water	2
	adhesion and cohesion	2
demonstrate	frozen water is less dense than liquid water	1
observe	water and describe what you see	1
diagram	the water cycle: evaporation, condensation, precipitation	3
design an experiment	to show the density of fresh water and saltwater	2
	to examine the properties of water, possibly including adhesion, cohesion, capillary action, surface tension, and solvency	any number
show cause and effect	of an ocean of water covering nearly three fourths of Earth's surface	2
	of water pressure	2
research	ways plants and animals have adapted to survive with little water	2
prove	the statement "Water is found on Earth in all three states of matter at the same time."	1
list	advantages and disadvantages of gravity moving water	2
	ways the human body uses water, including tears, lymph fluid, saliva, blood, urine, and sweat	6
identify	the hydrosphere as all bodies of water, ice, and the water in the atmosphere	3
graph	the percentage of water covering Earth's surface: 70.8% water, 29.2% land	2
	percentages of water in living organisms, possibly including jellyfish, frogs, human bodies, and dogs	any number
determine	what mercury and water have in common	2
outline	steps for extracting freshwater from salt water	2
write	about the importance of water to past, present, and future civilizations and development	3

Weather

Skill	Activity Suggestion	Foldable Part
question	create a "know?-like to know? -learned" about weather	3
chart	ways in which weather affects life	any number
research	common weather myths and corresponding science facts	2
compare and contrast	Earth's ocean of water and ocean of air	2
	weather and climate	2
	predicted and actual weather conditions	2
	heat and temperature	2
describe	the events before, during, and after a weather disaster in your community, possibly including a blizzard, flood, windstorm, ice storm, tornado, others	3
diagram	and describe the greenhouse effect	2
explain	the effect of weather on commercial planes, space shuttle missions, military operations, commerce, others	any number
graph	weather data by weeks, months, and years	3
illustrate	weather map symbols and label each	any number
	a convection current and explain how it influences weather	any number
make a table	to record daily and weekly weather, possibly including temperature, wind, cloud cover, sunrise time, sunset time, precipitation, others	any number
make a time line	of the history of meteorology	any number
research	the importance of satellites to weather forecasting	any number
	the layers of Earth's atmosphere as they relate to weather, including information about the troposphere	1
	two unusual weather phenomena, possibly including sun dogs and sun or moon halos	2
	the causes and effects of El Nino on weather	2
	weather Internet sites that provide worldwide forecasts	any number
sequence	the events of a weather forecast	any number
investigate	the causes and effects of the Dust Bowl, 1930's	2

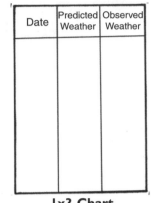

Date	Predicted Weather	Observed Weather

1x3 Chart

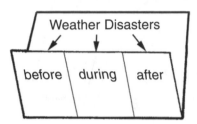

Weather Disasters

before | during | after

Three-tab concept map

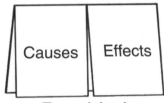

Causes | Effects

Two-tab book

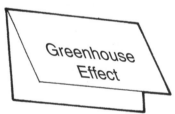

Greenhouse Effect

Half book

Weathering and Erosion

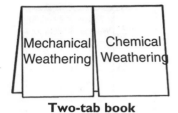

Two-tab book

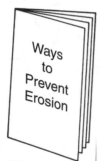

Shutter-fold book

Ways to Prevent Erosion

Bound book

Display case

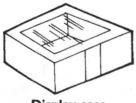

Skill	Activity Suggestion	Foldable Parts
question	create a "know?-like to know? -learned" about weather	3
compare and contrast	weathering and erosion	2
	mechanical and chemical weathering	2
determine	how effective different kinds of plants are at preventing erosion and holding soil, including trees, grass, and legumes	any number
debate	the pros and cons of trying to prevent erosion	2
describe	weathering as deterioration or breaking of parent rock into smaller pieces	1
	a land formation before and after weathering	2
	how soil formation depends on the environment, including time, climate, parent rock, surface of land, and living organisms in an area	any number
determine	agents of three weathering, including ice, water, acids, plant roots, temperature changes	3
explain	how soils are formed and destroyed	2
research	two changes in Earth's surface, including weathering, erosion, mass movement, changes in the crust, others	2
	what flowing and dripping water can do to rock	2
	two farming techniques that reduce erosion	2
	the "who, what, when, where" of John Wesley Powell	4
show cause and effect	of droughts on weathering and erosion	2

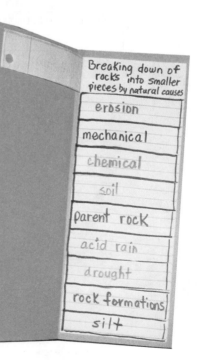

Wind

Skill	Activity Suggestion	Foldable Parts
question	create a "know?-like to know? -learned" about wind	3
observe	and record wind and its movement	1
	wind socks	1
	the wind as a force that causes movement, including flags, sails, windmills, tree limbs, others	1
chart	Beaufort's wind scale	any number
draw	and label windward and leeward	2
describe	the wind as a renewable energy source	1
	air masses	1
design	your own wind measurement scale	any number
	a wind vane and describe how it works	2
	wind chimes	1
locate	Earth's primary wind belts on a globe	1
make a table	to record direction and velocity of wind for a given time	2
	of world wind information, possibly including name, location, hot or cold, and season	any number
make a time line	showing the use of wind-generated energy	any number
research	instruments used to measure wind speed	any number
	gliders and hot air balloons	2
explain	cold fronts, stationary fronts, and warm fronts	3

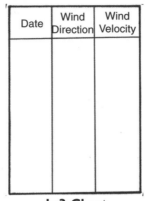

1x3 Chart

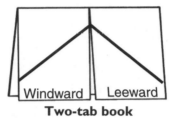

Two-tab book

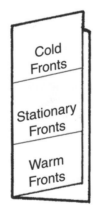

Three-tab book

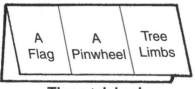

Three-tab book

Science
Graphics
and
Activities

Science Graphics

Earth Science

Life Science

Physical Science

Earth's Atmosphere

Use with Layered-Look Book

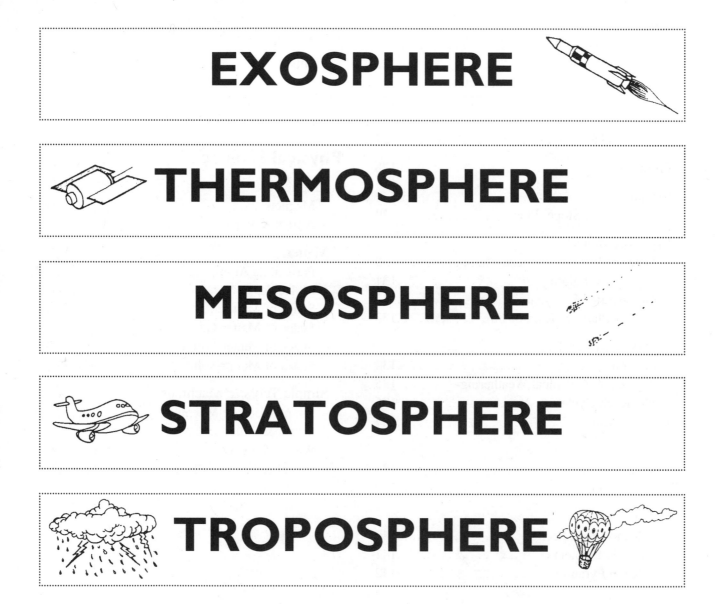

EXOSPHERE

THERMOSPHERE

MESOSPHERE

STRATOSPHERE

TROPOSPHERE

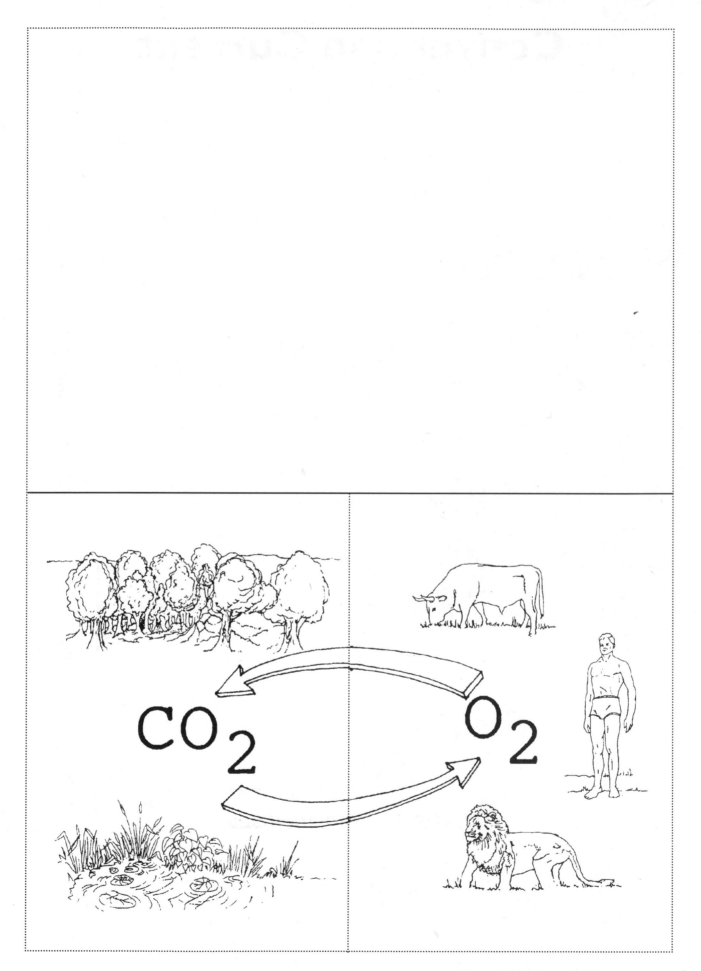

Convection Current

Folds into a Pyramid

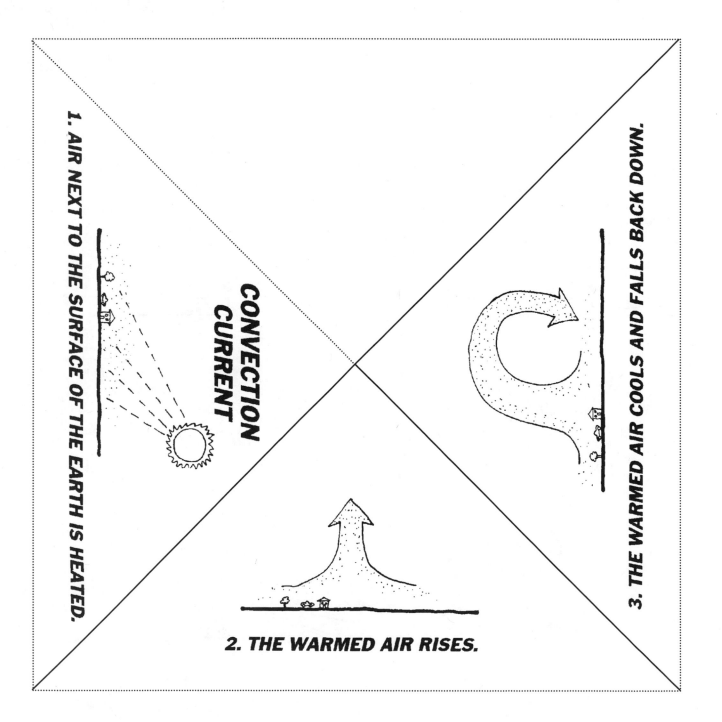

1. AIR NEXT TO THE SURFACE OF THE EARTH IS HEATED.

CONVECTION CURRENT

2. THE WARMED AIR RISES.

3. THE WARMED AIR COOLS AND FALLS BACK DOWN.

Clouds

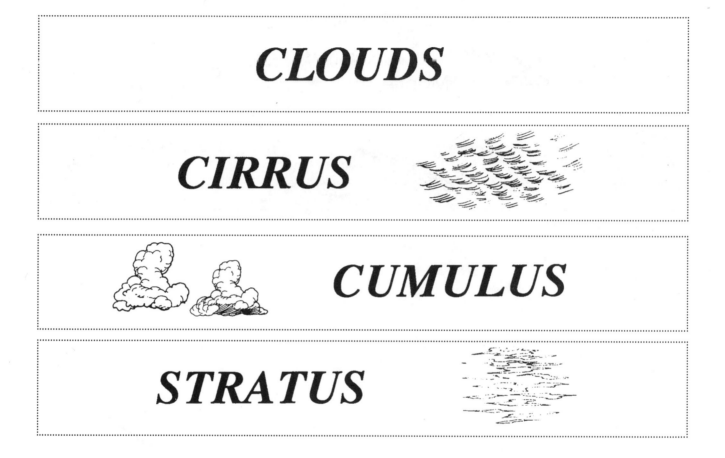

CLOUDS

CIRRUS

CUMULUS

STRATUS

Earth-Inside & Out

Folds into a Trifold Book

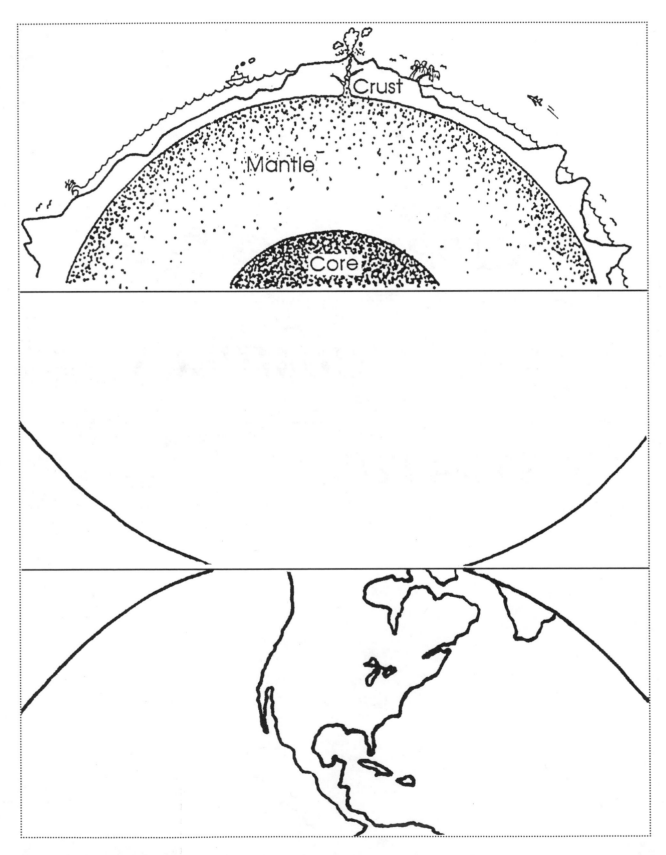

Crust

Mantle

Core

Layers of Earth

Use with Layered-Look Book

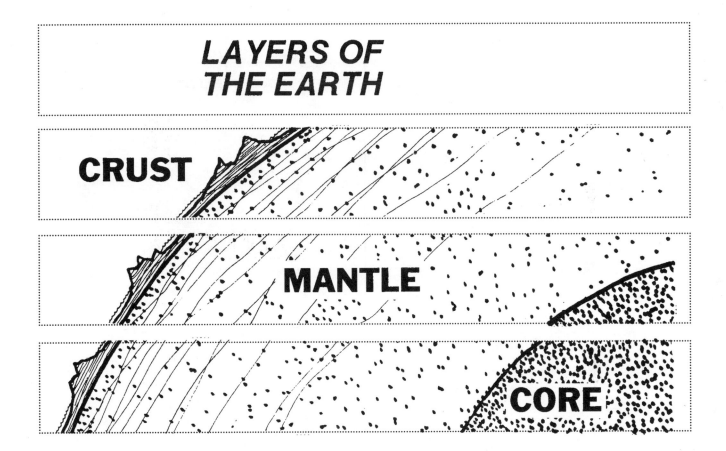

LAYERS OF
THE EARTH

CRUST

MANTLE

CORE

Landforms

Folds into a Four-tab Book

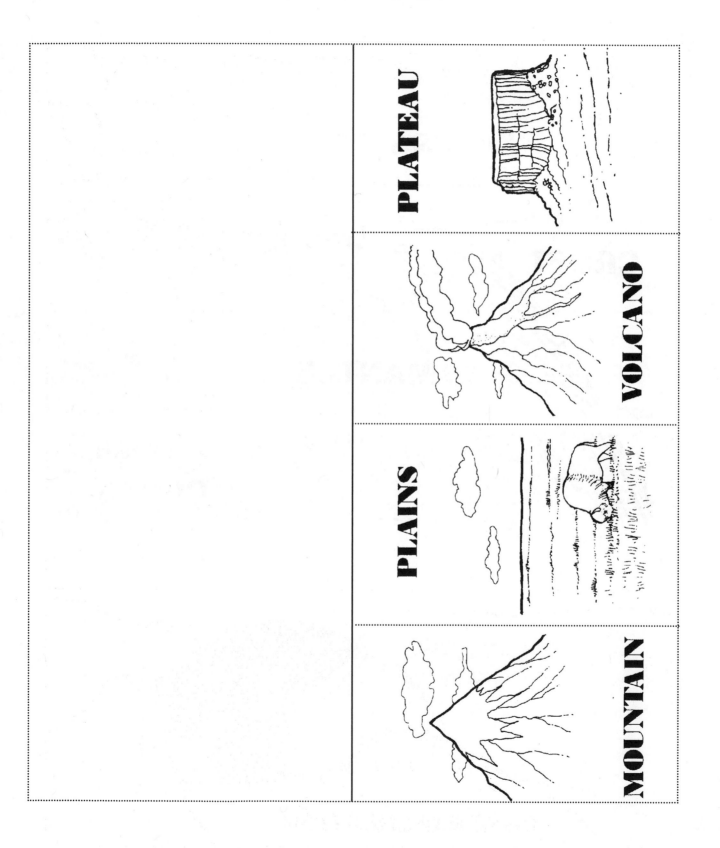

Caves

Folds into a Trifold Book

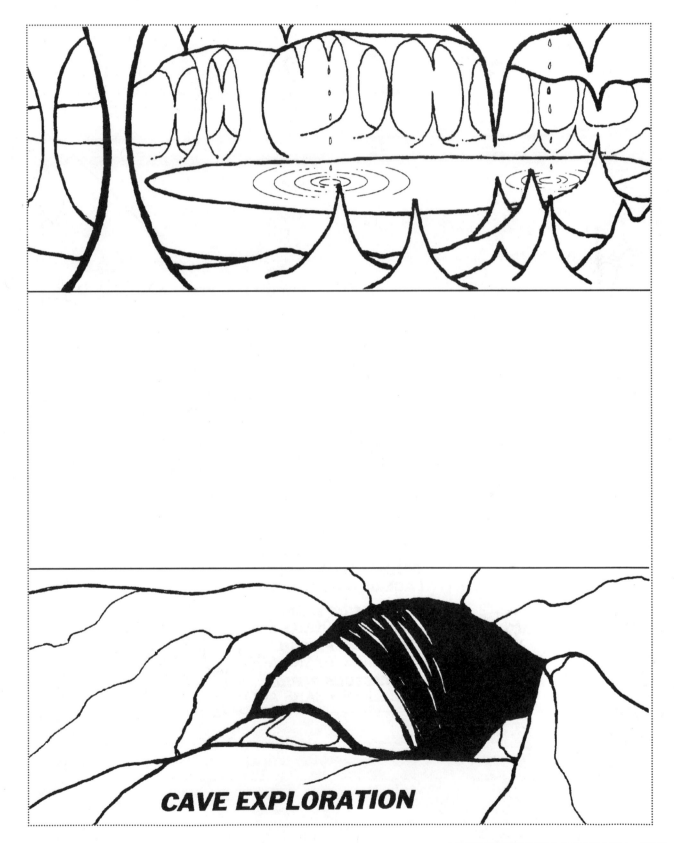

CAVE EXPLORATION

Geological Time

Folds into a Pyramid Fold

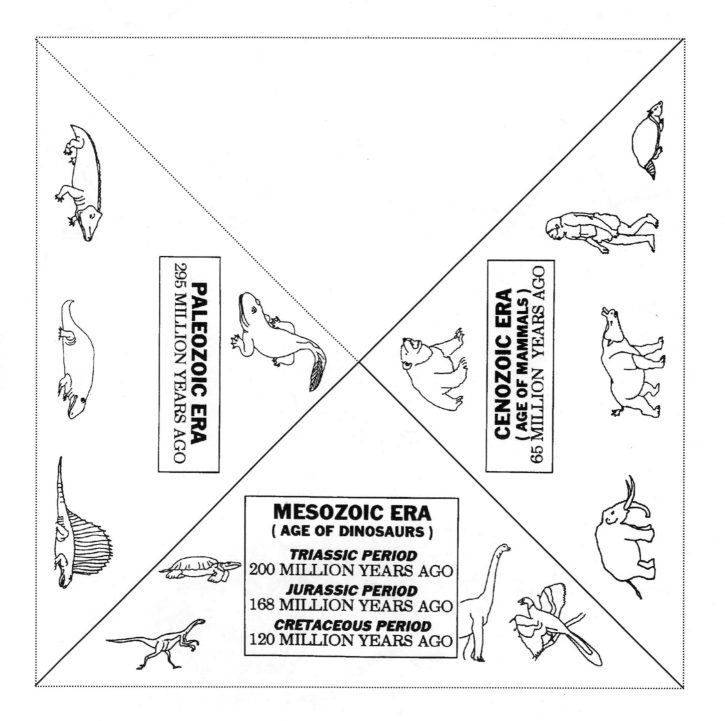

PALEOZOIC ERA
295 MILLION YEARS AGO

CENOZOIC ERA
(AGE OF MAMMALS)
65 MILLION YEARS AGO

MESOZOIC ERA
(AGE OF DINOSAURS)

TRIASSIC PERIOD
200 MILLION YEARS AGO
JURASSIC PERIOD
168 MILLION YEARS AGO
CRETACEOUS PERIOD
120 MILLION YEARS AGO

Plate Movement

Use with Three-tab Book

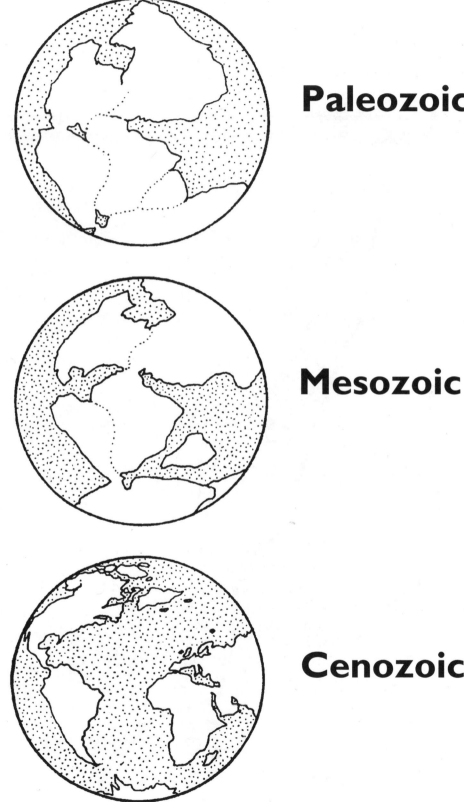

Paleozoic

Mesozoic

Cenozoic

Glaciers

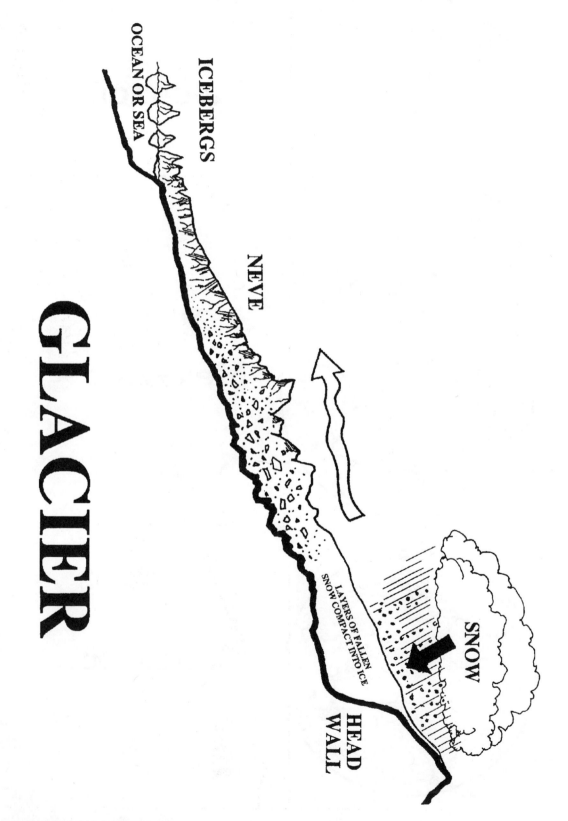

OCEAN OR SEA

ICEBERGS

NEVE

GLACIER

LAYERS OF FALLEN SNOW COMPACT INTO ICE

SNOW

HEAD WALL

Land, Shelf, Slope, & Floor

Folds into a Four-tab Book

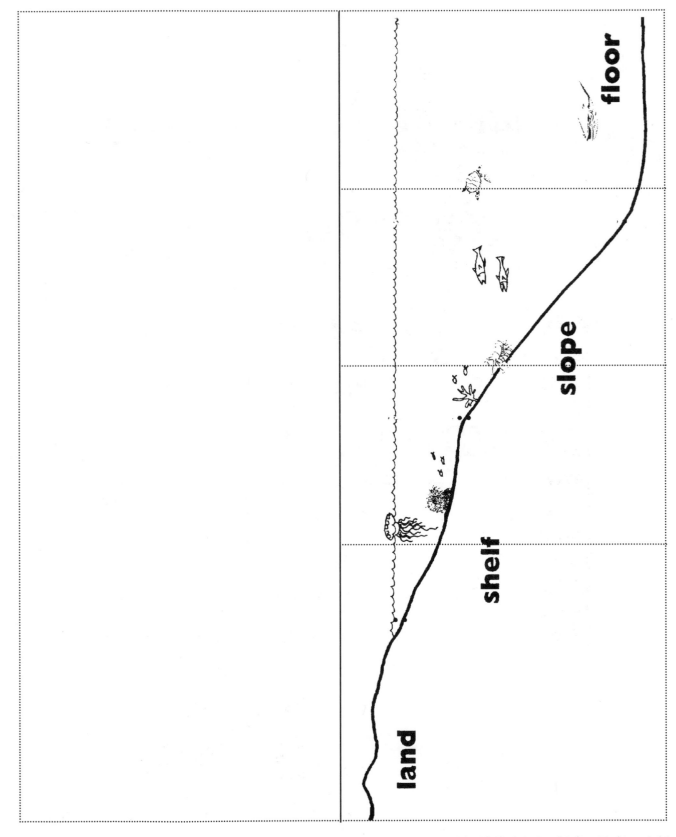

Types of Plate Movement

Use with Layered-Look Book

Plates Move Three Ways

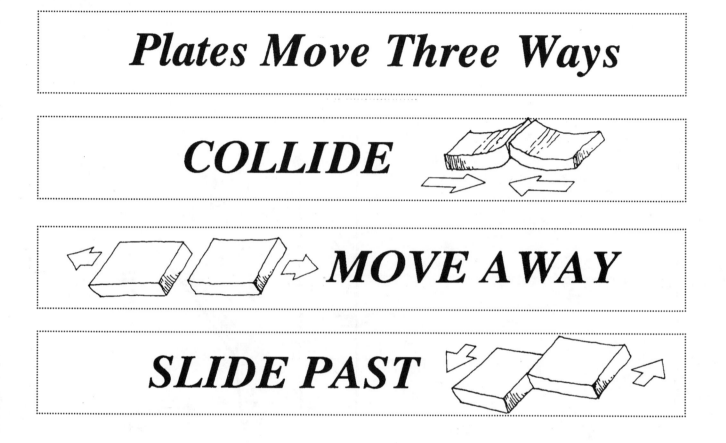

COLLIDE

MOVE AWAY

SLIDE PAST

faulting

folding

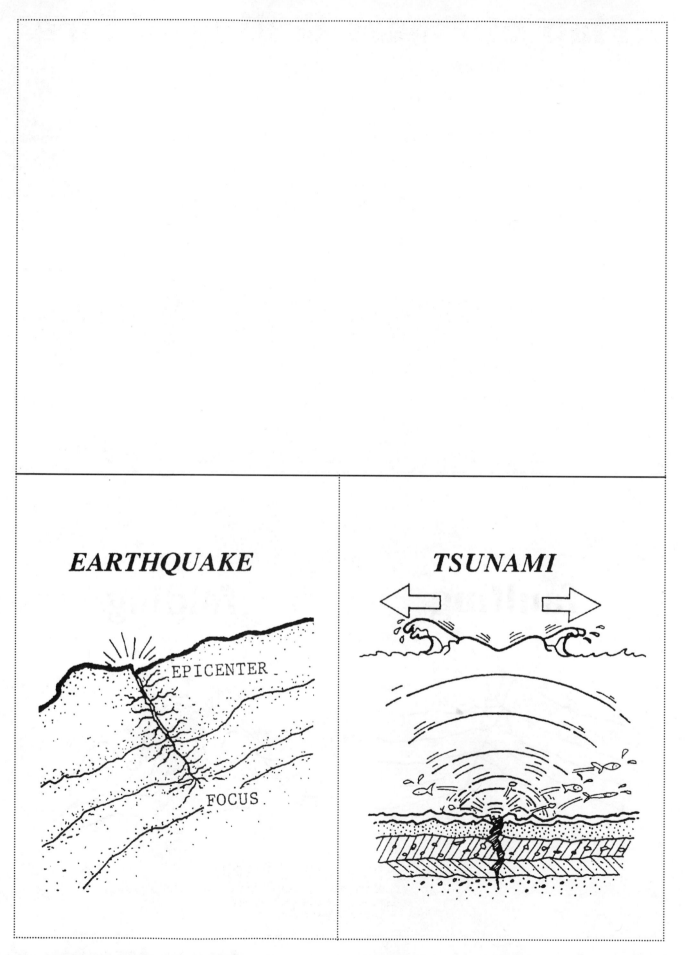

EARTHQUAKE

EPICENTER

FOCUS

TSUNAMI

Map of Plates & Ring of Fire

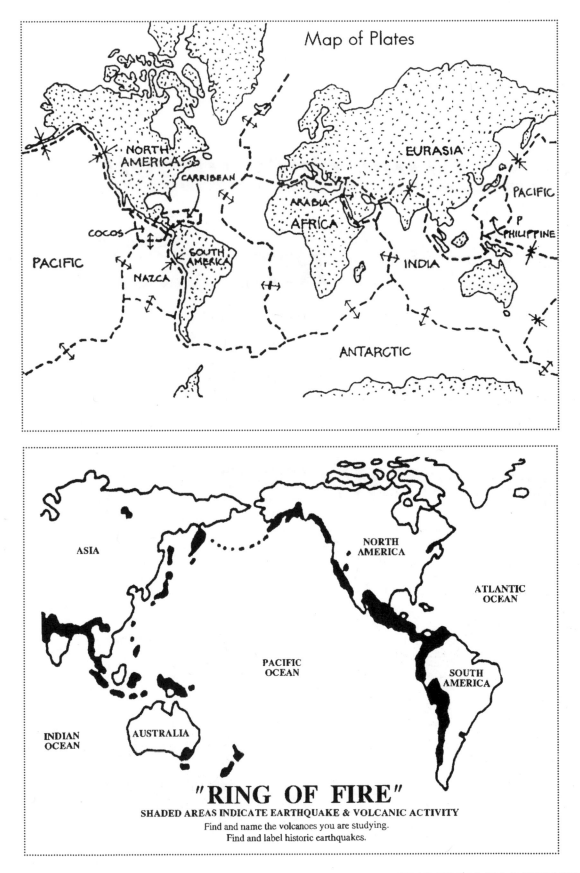

Map of Plates

NORTH AMERICA

CARRIBEAN

COCOS

PACIFIC

NAZCA

SOUTH AMERICA

EURASIA

ARABIA

AFRICA

PACIFIC

P PHILIPPINE

INDIA

ANTARCTIC

ASIA

NORTH AMERICA

ATLANTIC OCEAN

PACIFIC OCEAN

SOUTH AMERICA

INDIAN OCEAN

AUSTRALIA

"RING OF FIRE"
SHADED AREAS INDICATE EARTHQUAKE & VOLCANIC ACTIVITY
Find and name the volcanoes you are studying.
Find and label historic earthquakes.

Erosion

From Rock to Soil

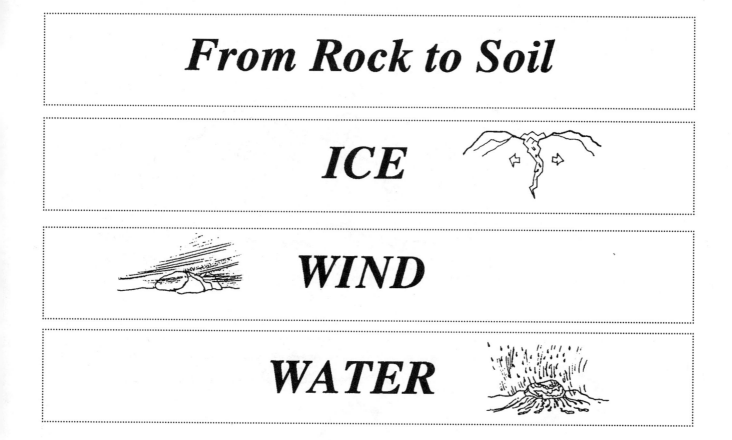

ICE

WIND

WATER

Physical & Chemical Weathering

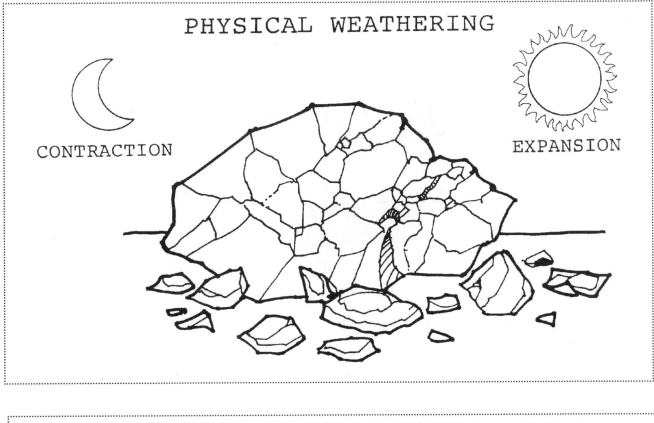

PHYSICAL WEATHERING

CONTRACTION

EXPANSION

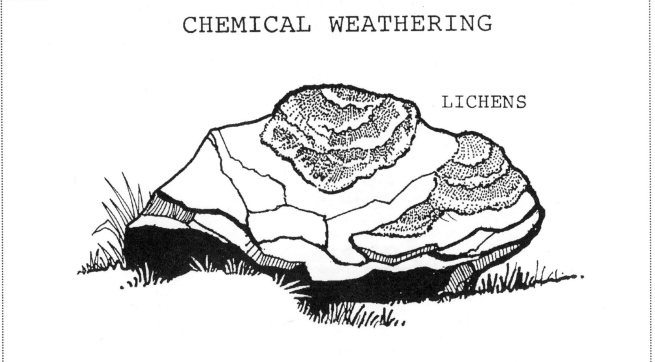

CHEMICAL WEATHERING

LICHENS

The Rock Cycle

Folds into a Pyramid

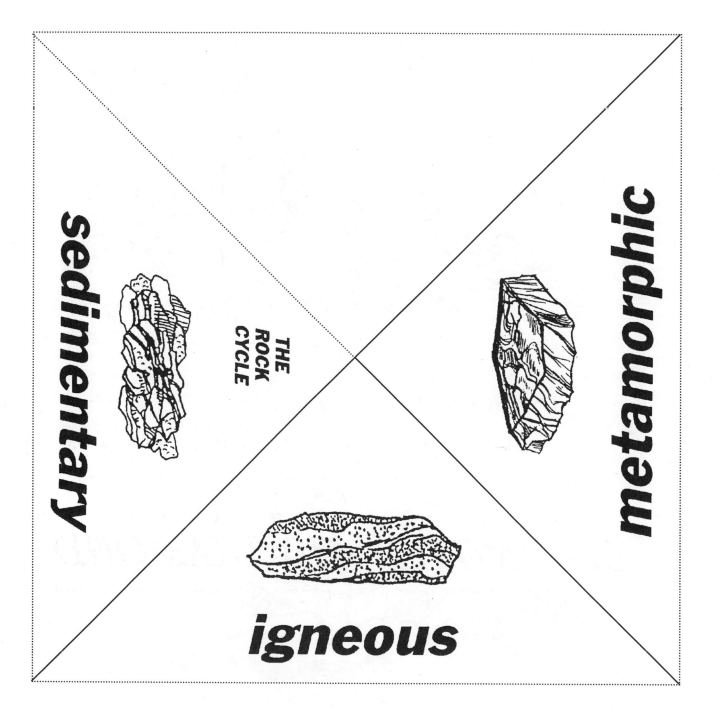

Moh's Scale

Use with Layered-Look Book

1. TALC	*6. ORTHOCLASE*
2. GYPSUM	*7. QUARTZ*
3. CALCITE	*8. TOPAZ*
4. FLUORITE	*9. CORUNDUM*
5. APATITE	*10. DIAMOND*

Solar System

Asteroids

Jupiter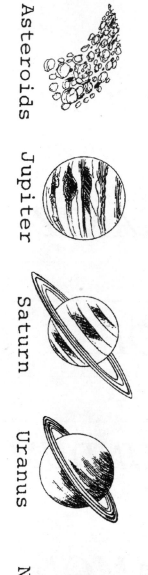

Saturn

Uranus

Neptune

Pluto

Galaxy

Sun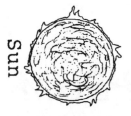

Mercury

Venus

Earth

Mars

Types of Galaxies

Folds into a Pyramid

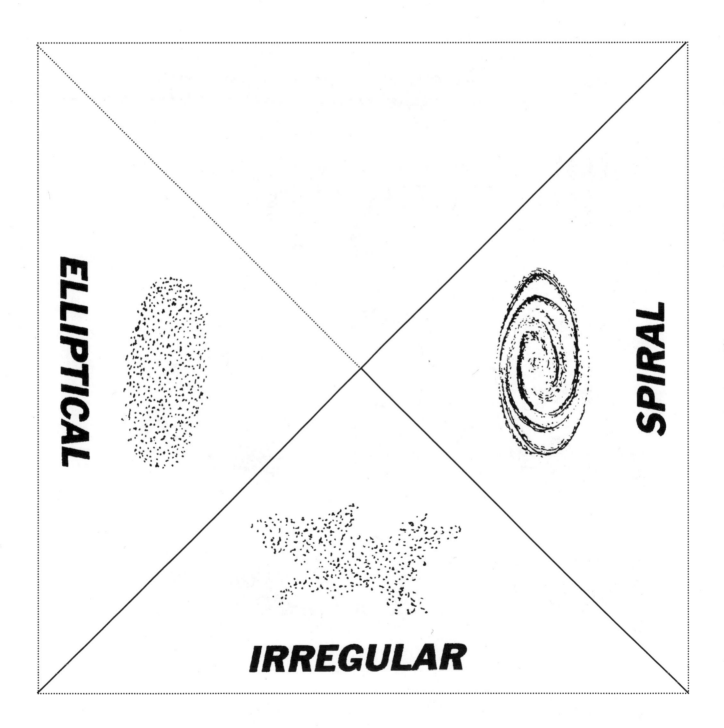

Volcano Cross-Section

Use with Layered-Look Book

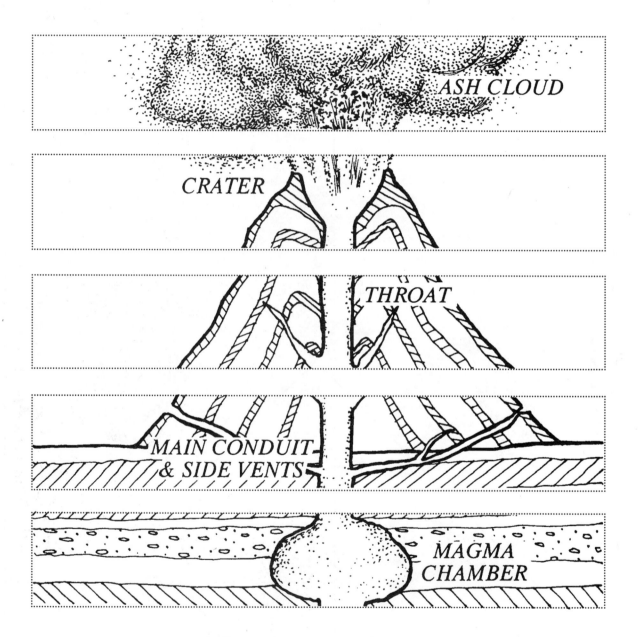

ASH CLOUD

CRATER

THROAT

MAIN CONDUIT & SIDE VENTS

MAGMA CHAMBER

Volcanic Elements

Folds into a Four-tab Book

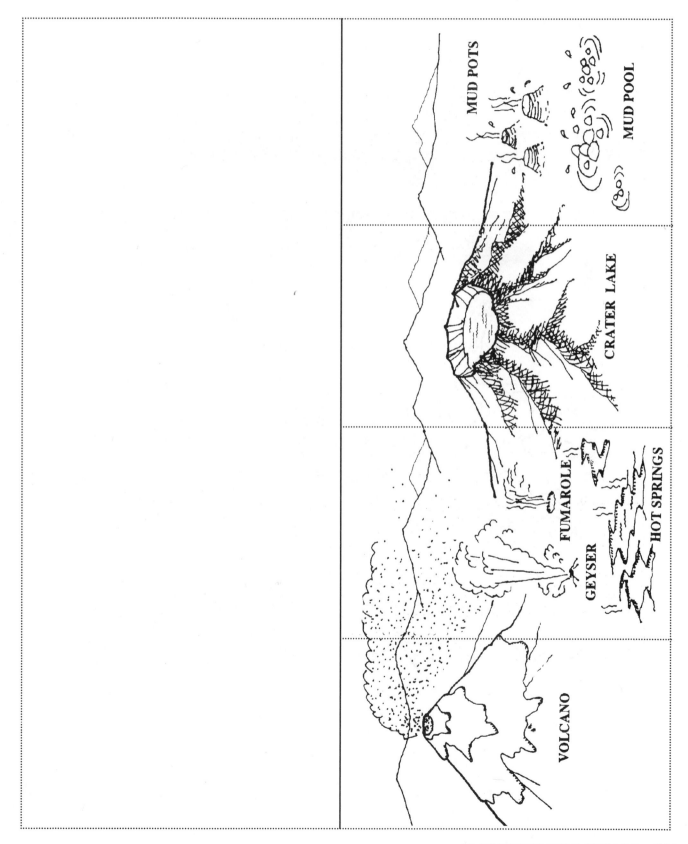

Volcano

Folds into a Pyramid Fold

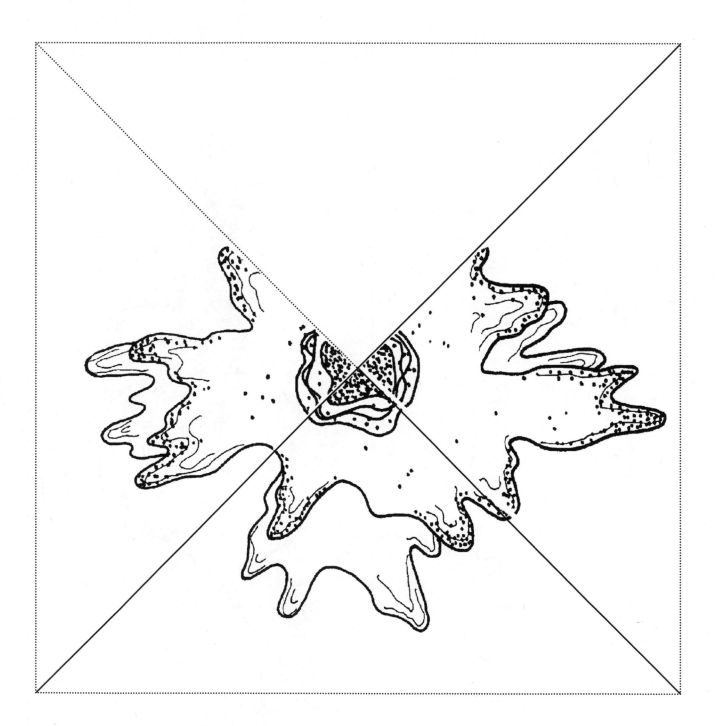

Nocturnal & Diurnal

Nocturnal Animals

Diurnal Animals

Herbivores, Omnivores, & Carnivores

Folds into a Three-tab Book

Growth & Development

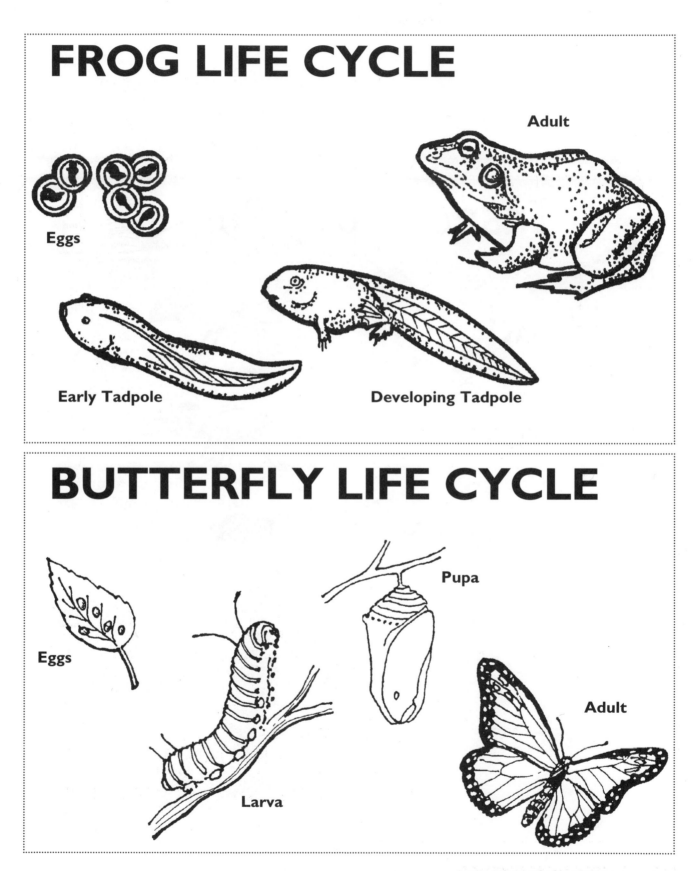

FROG LIFE CYCLE

Eggs

Early Tadpole

Developing Tadpole

Adult

BUTTERFLY LIFE CYCLE

Eggs

Larva

Pupa

Adult

Insect Body Parts

Use with Layered-Look Book

Insect Body Parts

Head

Thorax

Abdomen

Incomplete Metamorphosis

Use With Layered-Look Book

Incomplete Metamorphosis

EGG

NYMPH

ADULT

Butterflies

Use with Butterfly Pyramid Mobile

Spiders & Bees

Use With Spider Web and Bee Colony Pyramid Mobiles

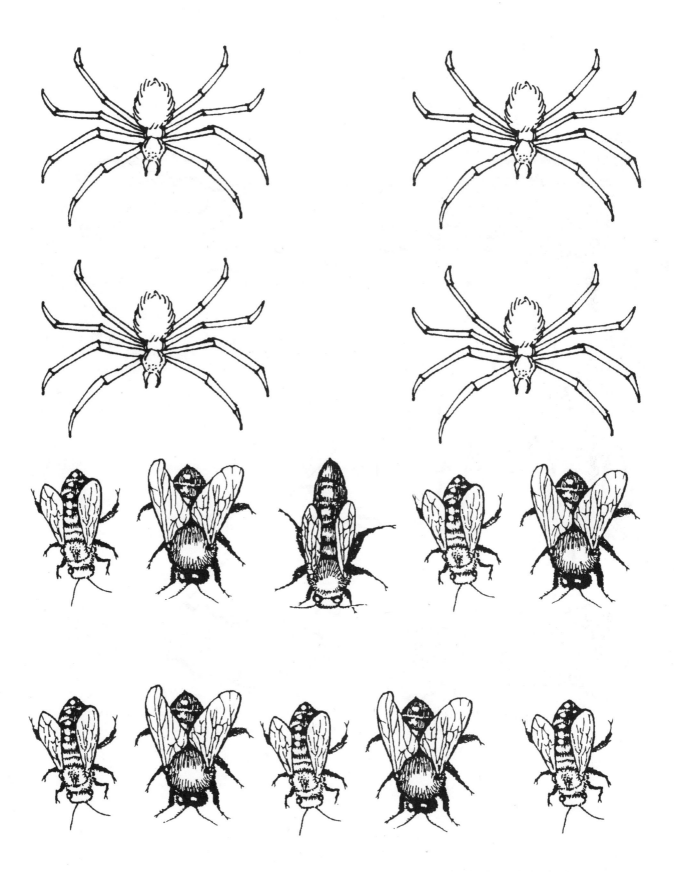

Butterflies

Folds into a Pyramid Mobile

Spider Web

Folds into a Pyramid Mobile

Bee Colony

Folds into a Pyramid Mobile

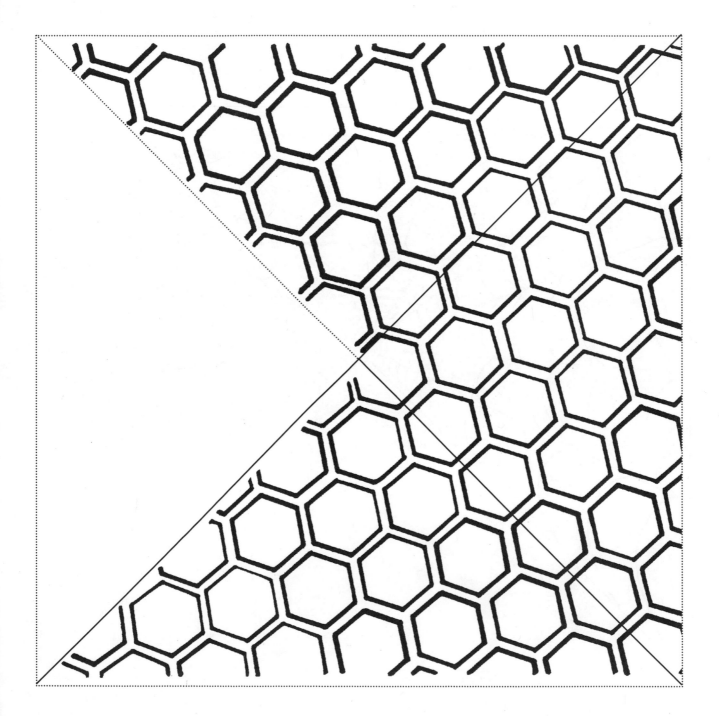

Ocean Life

Use with Layered-Look Book

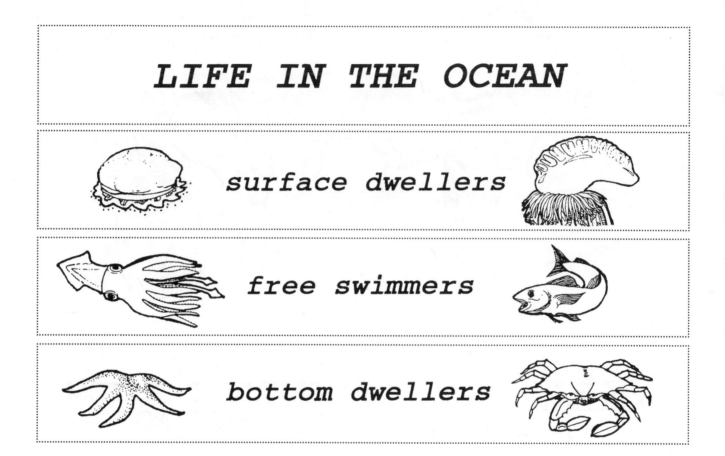

LIFE IN THE OCEAN

surface dwellers

free swimmers

bottom dwellers

Muscular & Skeletal Systems

Use with Four-door Book

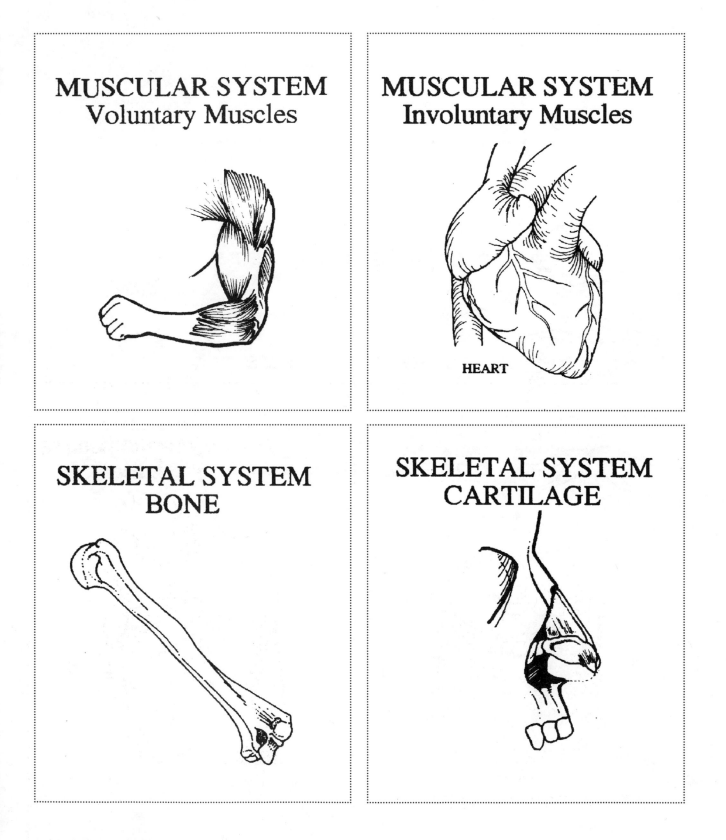

MUSCULAR SYSTEM
Voluntary Muscles

MUSCULAR SYSTEM
Involuntary Muscles

HEART

SKELETAL SYSTEM
BONE

SKELETAL SYSTEM
CARTILAGE

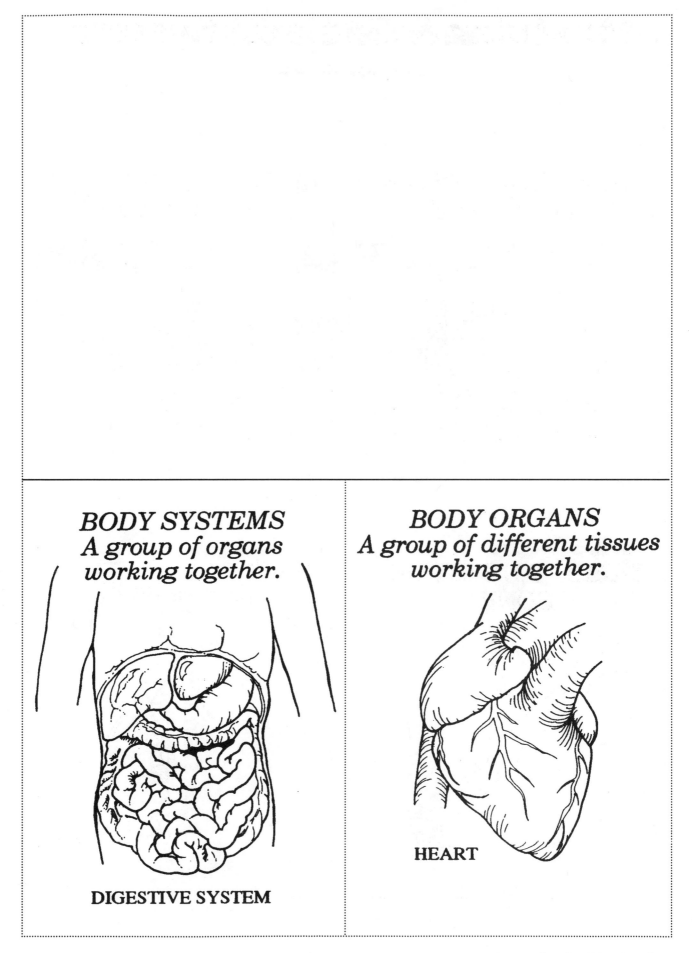

BODY SYSTEMS
A group of organs working together.

DIGESTIVE SYSTEM

BODY ORGANS
A group of different tissues working together.

HEART

Human Body Systems

Use with Pocket Books

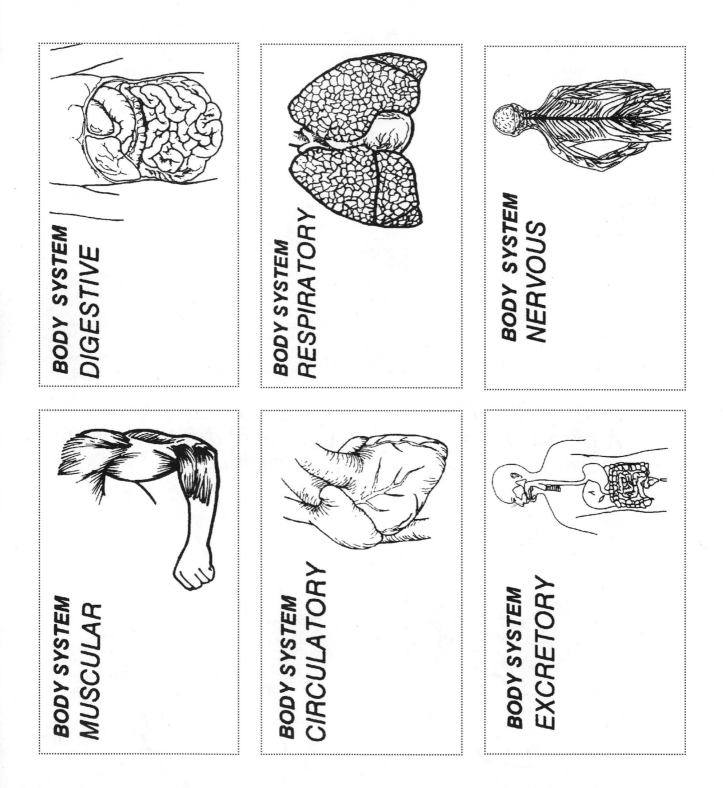

BODY SYSTEM
DIGESTIVE

BODY SYSTEM
RESPIRATORY

BODY SYSTEM
NERVOUS

BODY SYSTEM
MUSCULAR

BODY SYSTEM
CIRCULATORY

BODY SYSTEM
EXCRETORY

Human Body Systems

Use with Pocket Books

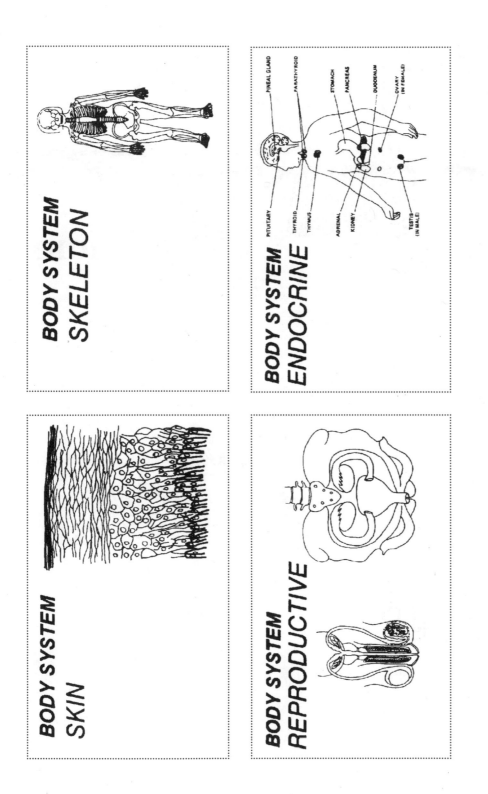

BODY SYSTEM
SKELETON

BODY SYSTEM
ENDOCRINE

PINEAL GLAND
PARATHYROID
STOMACH
PANCREAS
DUODENUM
OVARY (IN FEMALE)
PITUITARY
THYROID
THYMUS
ADRENAL
KIDNEY
TESTIS (IN MALE)

BODY SYSTEM
SKIN

BODY SYSTEM
REPRODUCTIVE

The Five Senses

Use with Pop-up Book

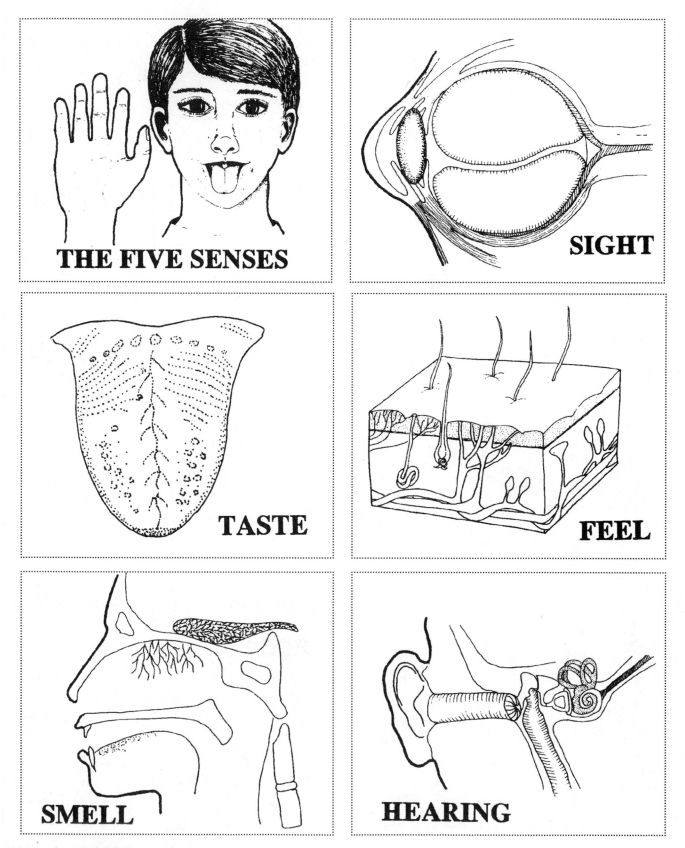

THE FIVE SENSES

SIGHT

TASTE

FEEL

SMELL

HEARING

Flowering Seed Plants

Folds into a Four-tab Book

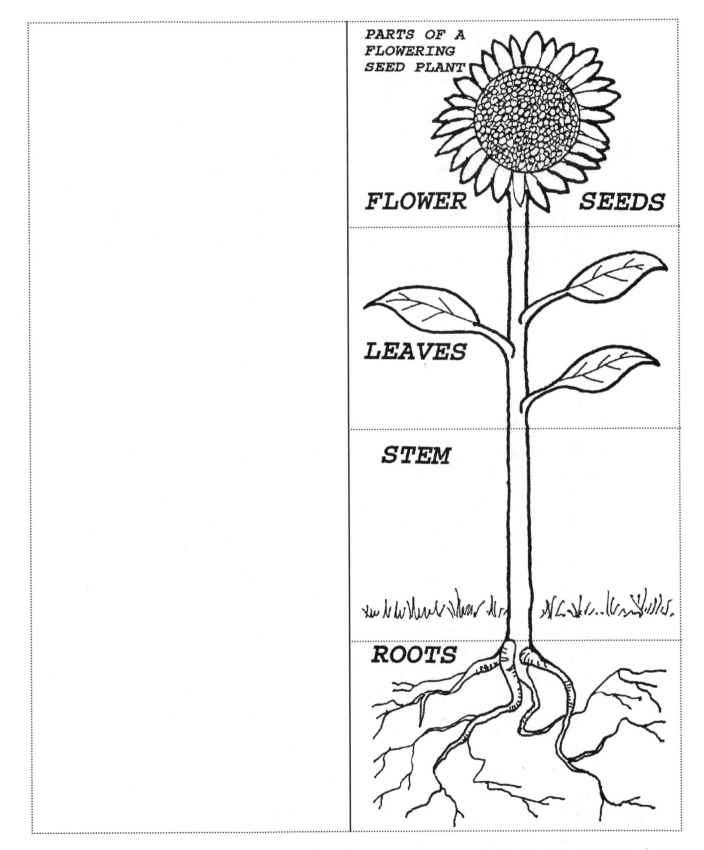

PARTS OF A
FLOWERING
SEED PLANT

FLOWER   SEEDS

LEAVES

STEM

ROOTS

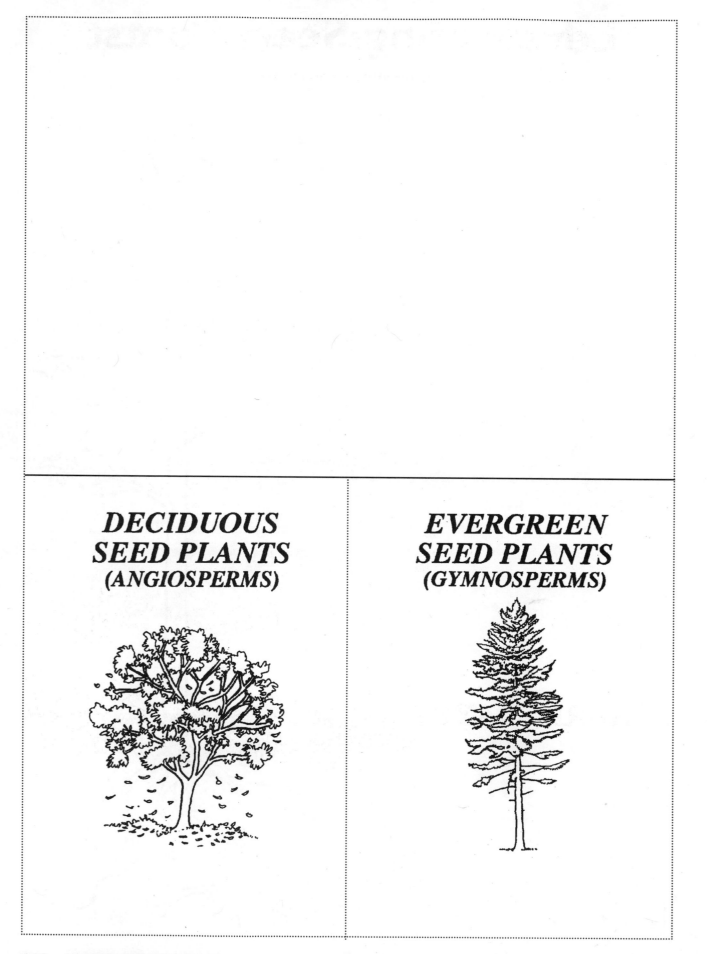

DECIDUOUS
SEED PLANTS
(ANGIOSPERMS)

EVERGREEN
SEED PLANTS
(GYMNOSPERMS)

Levels of the Rain Forest

Use With Layered-Look Book

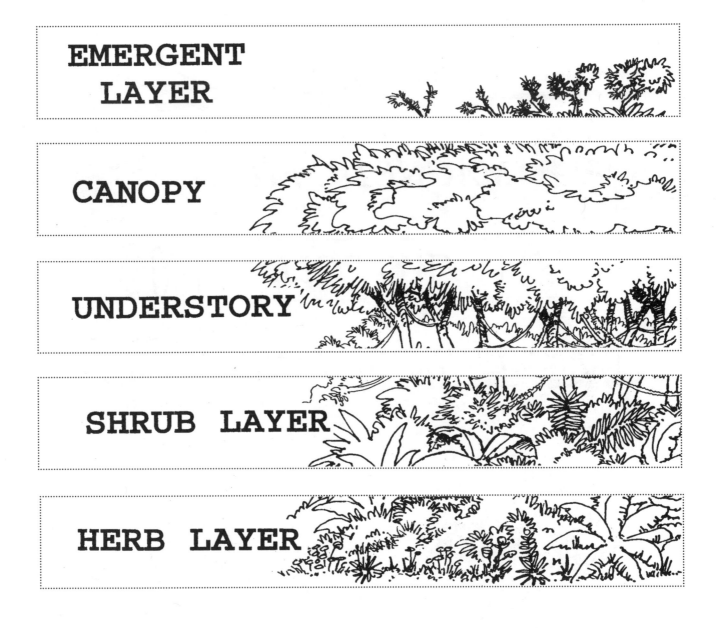

EMERGENT LAYER

CANOPY

UNDERSTORY

SHRUB LAYER

HERB LAYER

Magnets

Use with Layered-Look Book

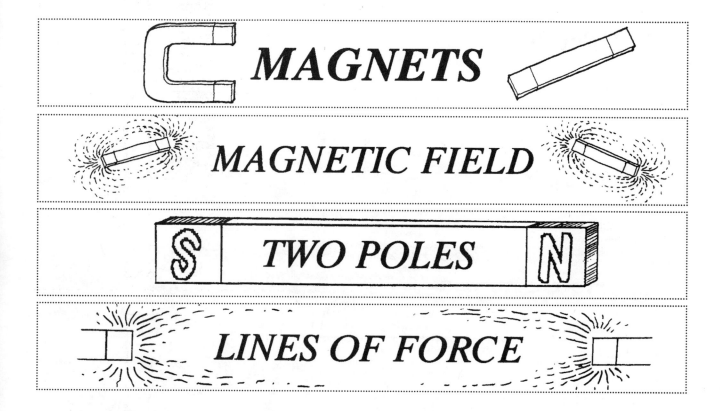

MAGNETS

MAGNETIC FIELD

TWO POLES

LINES OF FORCE

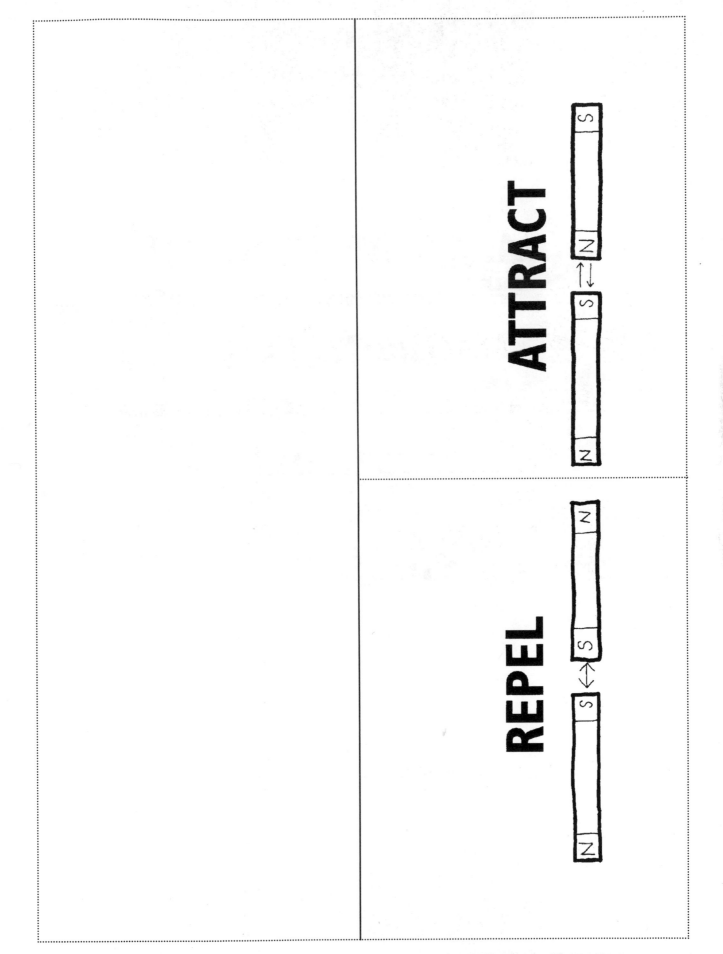

Parts of an Atom

Use with Layered-Look Book or Pyramid Fold

PARTS OF AN ATOM

protons

neutrons

electrons

Molecules

Use with Layered-Look Book or Pyramid Fold

Molecules

Mixtures

Compounds

Elements

Four States of Matter

Use with Layered-Look Book

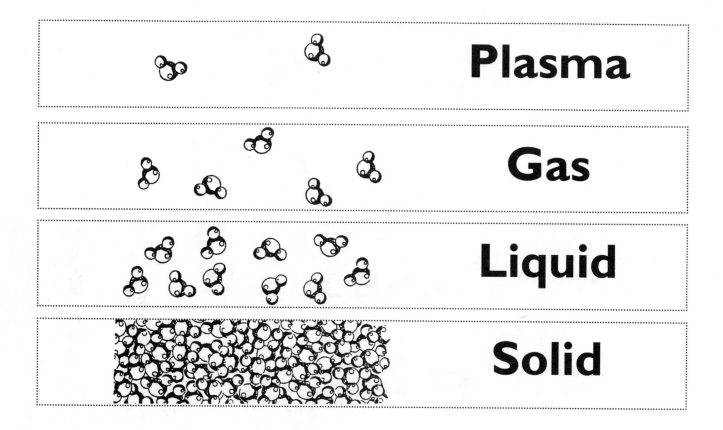

Plasma

Gas

Liquid

Solid

States of Matter-Gas

Folds into a Trifold Book

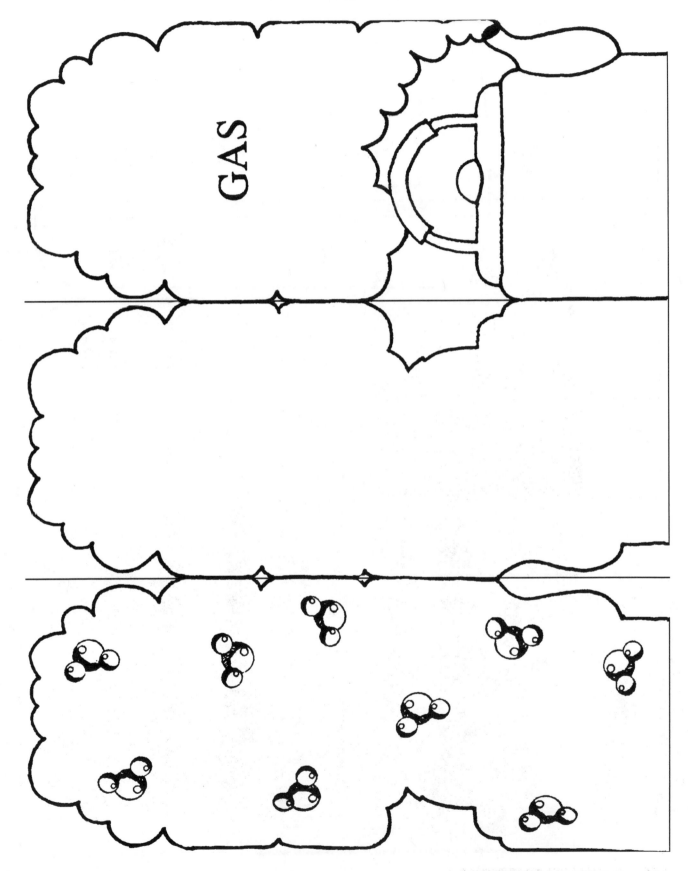

States of Matter-Liquid

Folds into a Trifold Book

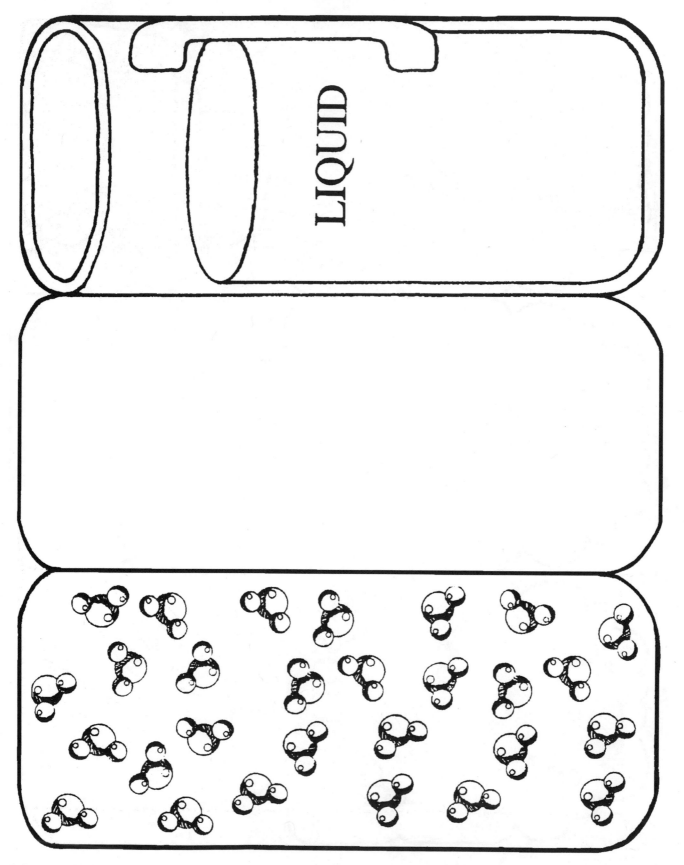

LIQUID

States of Matter-Solid

Folds into a Trifold Book

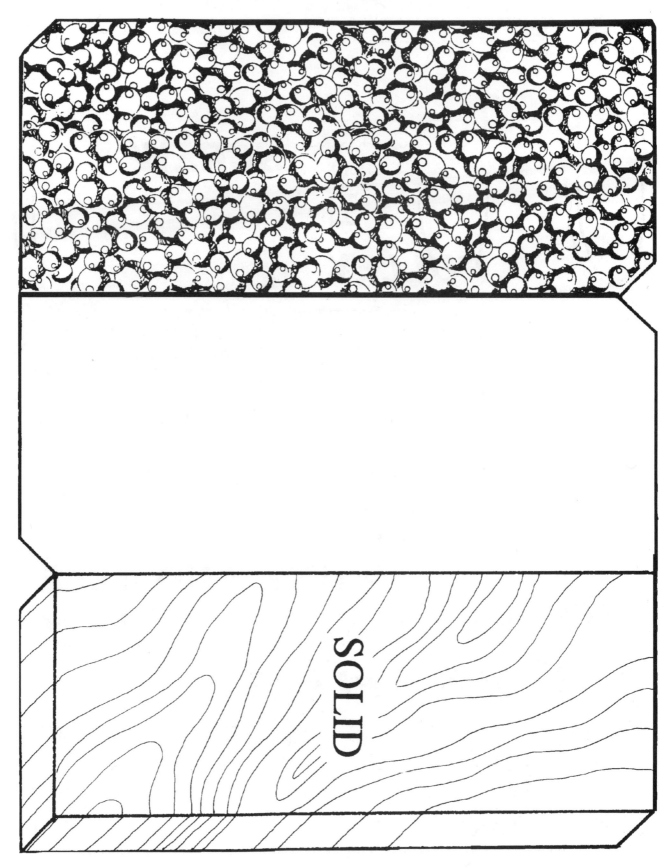

Simple Tools & Machines

Use with Layered-Look Book

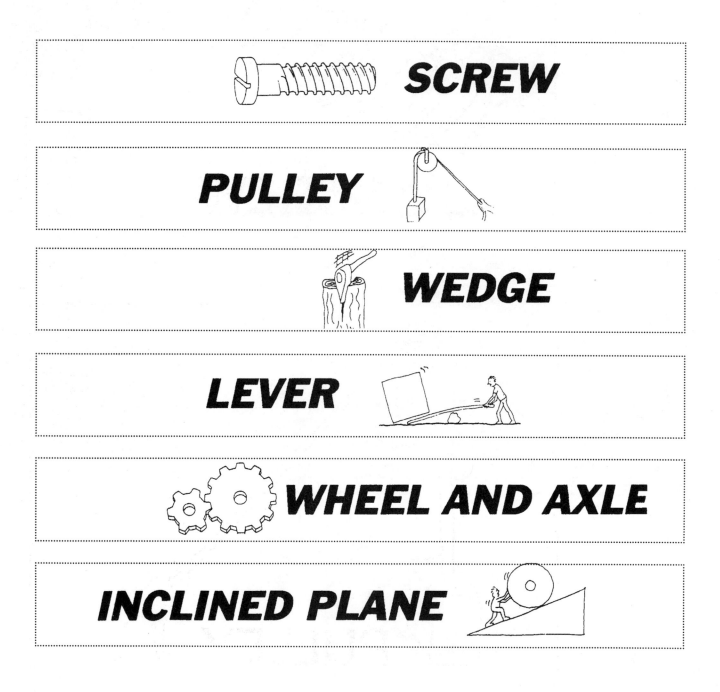

SCREW

PULLEY

WEDGE

LEVER

WHEEL AND AXLE

INCLINED PLANE

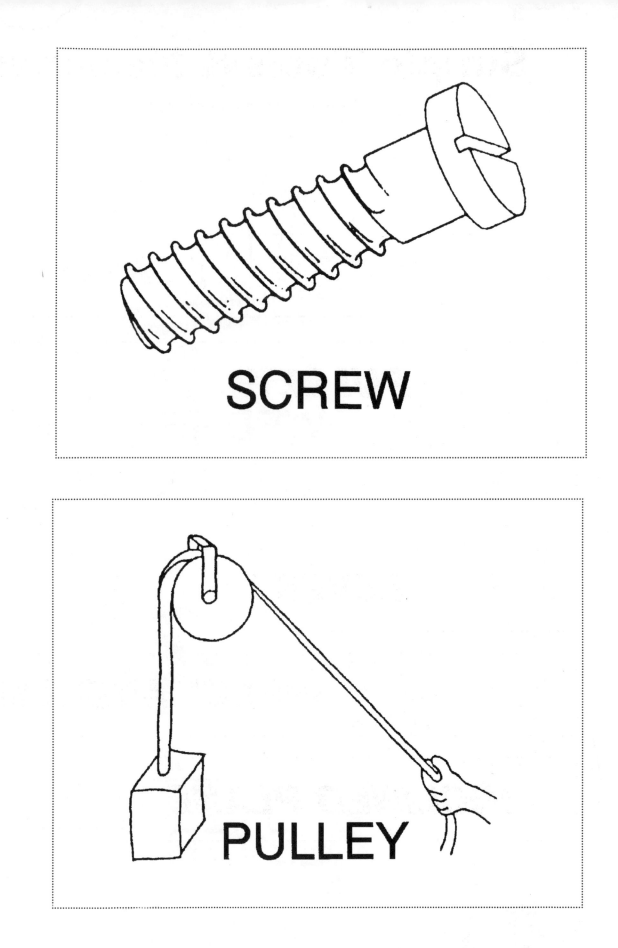

SCREW

PULLEY

WEDGE

LEVER

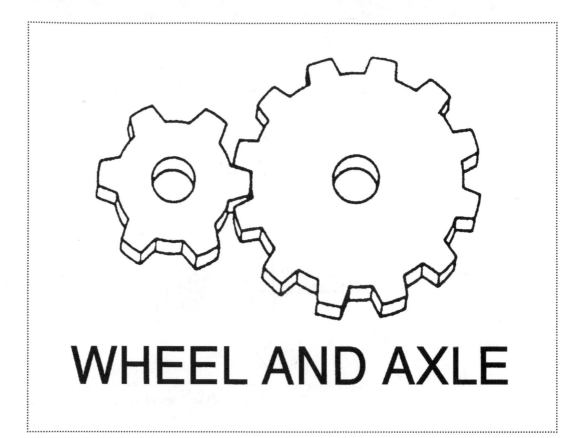

WHEEL AND AXLE

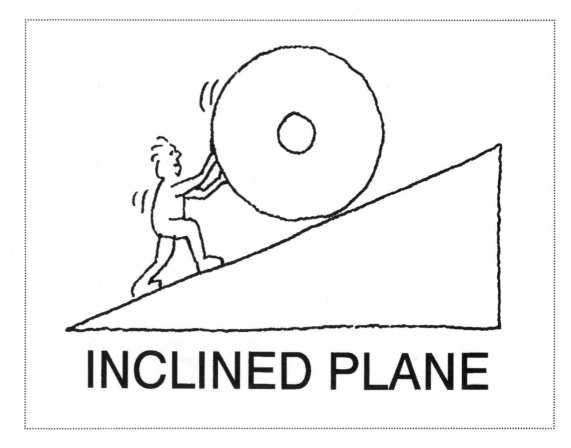

INCLINED PLANE

Index

Index

Workshops and Keynote Presentations

Dinah's presentations give participants an unprecedented opportunity to meet and work with the designer as she shares her internationally renowned, three-dimensional, interactive graphic organizers. Teachers learn how to make class work, projects, assessment, and note taking unforgettable visual and kinesthetic experiences. Dinah's Foldables™ can be used by students and teachers in all grade levels and subjects.

Workshops

For more information on Dinah Zike's workshops and keynote presentations, contact Cecile Stepman at **1-210-698-0123** or **cecile@dinah.com**.

Orders

To receive a free catalog or to order other books by Dinah Zike, call **1-800-99DINAH** or email at **orders@dinah.com**.

E-Group

To join Dinah Zike's e-group and receive new activity ideas, send an email to **mindy@dinah.com** or sign up on our website at **www.dinah.com**.

Watch for new and upcoming books in
Dinah Zike's Big Book series!

Each book in Dinah's Big Book series is subject specific and features instructions for approximately thirty graphic organizers, 100 full-color photographed examples, five black-line art examples per page, and thousands of graphic organizer ideas for teaching.

Please check our website at www.dinah.com or call 210-698-0123 for availability of books for the following subjects:

Elementary
Dinah Zike's Big Book of...
Social Studies (K-6)
Texas History (K-7)
Math (K-6)
Science (K-6)
Classroom Organization (general)
Phonics, Spelling, and Vocabulary

Middle School and High School
Dinah Zike's Big Book of...
Science (7-12)
Math (7-12)
American History (7-12)
World History (7-12)